Contents

We deliberately haven't put any _essay_ answers in this book, because they'd just be repeating what's in the revision guide. Instead, we've put in a section about how to write good essay answers, and do well. Answers for the _numerical_ questions are included though, on page 102.

What Businesses Do

Businesses are everywhere. There are businesses around that do pretty much anything you care to mention.
Although businesses are varied, most of them have plenty in common. **These two pages are for AQA, OCR and Edexcel.**

Businesses *usually exist to* Make a Profit

1) Businesses have to **make a profit** to survive.
   Profit means a business is **gaining** more money than it's **spending**.

Public sector = government-owned.
Private sector = privately owned.

2) This is especially true in the **private sector**, where if a business doesn't make
   enough money to survive it could go **bankrupt** and have to **close down**.

3) In the **public sector**, things aren't as clear cut. Organisations like the army, the police, hospitals
   and state schools aren't there to **make money** — they exist to provide a service to the community.

4) **Charities** are another exception — they don't exist to make a profit. But they do need enough income
   to **cover their costs** — and sometimes to generate a small surplus to put back into the business.

5) As well as making a profit, businesses may have **other objectives** such as:

   - Offering the **highest quality** goods and services possible.
   - Increasing their **market share**.
   - Giving good **customer service**.
   - Having a good **image** and **reputation**.
   - Trying to limit their **impact** on the **environment**.

   Market share is how much of the market a firm has compared to its competitors.

6) Businesses might **give up some profit** to help them meet **other objectives**. However, most
   company owners are **ultimately** only interested in **profit**. Everything else comes **after**.

Businesses *also have to meet the* Needs *of* Stakeholders

Everyone who is affected by a business is called a **stakeholder**.
There are two types: **internal** stakeholders and **external** stakeholders.

Shareholders can be company directors, or people outside the business who hold shares.

INTERNAL STAKEHOLDERS — People inside the business

1) The **owners** are the most important stakeholders. They make a profit if the business is successful and
   decide what happens to the business. In a limited company, the **shareholders** are the owners.

2) **Employees** are interested in their **job security** and **promotion** prospects. They also want to earn a
   decent wage and have **pleasant working conditions**. **Managers** have **extra concerns** — they'll probably
   get some of the blame if the company does badly, and some of the credit if things go well.

EXTERNAL STAKEHOLDERS — People outside the business

1) **Customers** want **high quality** products at **low prices**.

2) **Suppliers** are the people and businesses who sell **raw materials** to the business.
   The business provides them with their **income**. If the business doesn't have enough
   money to pay them quickly enough, the suppliers can have **cash flow** problems.

3) Most businesses are run on **credit**. **Creditors** (people who are owed money by the
   business) have a stake in the business. They want to make sure they get paid on time.
   In some cases, they may want check up on a business to make sure it's **creditworthy**.

4) The **local community** will **gain** if the business provides **local employment** and **sponsors** local activities.
   The community will **suffer** if the business causes noise and pollution, or if the business has to **cut jobs**.

5) The **government** gets more in **taxes** when the business makes good profits.

A business is **accountable** to its stakeholders. It has to satisfy their needs and answer their criticisms.
However, some stakeholders are **more important** to the business than others (see p.84-85).

1) A business can't ignore its **customers**. If the business **can't sell its products**, it'll go **bust**.

2) No limited company can afford to ignore its **shareholders**. If they're unhappy with
   the way things are run, they can **sack the directors** or **sell** the business to **someone else**.

What Businesses Do

Businesses all need certain Key Things

Before businesses can sell things and make a profit, they need certain things.

There's more on different sources of finance on p.40-41.

1)	**Labour**	Businesses need people to do the work.
2)	**Finance**	It costs money to provide goods and services.
3)	**Customers**	Every business needs people to buy the goods and services, and pay for them.
4)	**Suppliers**	Suppliers provide raw materials, equipment and human resources.
5)	**Premises**	Businesses need buildings to work in.
6)	**Enterprise**	Entrepreneurs come up with original ideas and take risks to make a profit.

A business needs **physical** resources such as raw materials and machines, **human** resources to do the work and **financial** resources to pay for everything. All these resources come together to produce goods and services.

Businesses all Do Certain Things to help them make Profit

Production of goods or services isn't enough on its own — businesses have a whole load of **other tasks** to do before they're likely to achieve the ultimate goal of **making a profit**. These different tasks are usually looked after by different departments.

Business departments and their roles

Finance	Businesses have to keep a careful eye on their finances. They must keep detailed and accurate **financial records**. A business must try to get the best **value for money** for every pound it spends.
HRM	**(Human Resources Management)** Businesses must make sure they have the right number of employees of the right quality in the right place at the right time.
Marketing	Businesses have to identify what customers **want** or **need** and figure out how best to **sell** it to them.
Admin	Businesses have to **run their own affairs** as efficiently as possible.
R&D	**(Research and Development)** Businesses may need to discover **new ideas** for products that might be wanted in the future, and get them ready to be launched onto the market.

1) Businesses need to **plan** what activities to do in the future.
2) They need to **control** what workers in the business are doing, and control the amount of money that's spent.
3) Businesses need to **coordinate** all their different functions and departments and make sure that all the departments are working towards common objectives.

Practice Questions

Q1 What objectives might a private sector business have? Which objective is the most important and why?

Q2 Who are the stakeholders in a business and why do they have an interest?

Q3 Name at least four essential things that a business needs to produce goods and services.

Q4 What is the role of an entrepreneur?

Exam Questions

Q1 Discuss the idea that businesses only exist to make a profit. (10 marks)

Q2 Describe the different types of stakeholder in a large company, and explain their importance to the company. (6 marks)

But does the steak holder come with a chips holder?

This first section covers fairly basic business ideas. If you've done GCSE Business Studies, some of it might seem a bit dull. Don't assume you already know it all though — it's worth reading through to make sure you really know what's what. Some of these things will crop up again later in the book — so stick with this section. And then go on to the good stuff...

Legal Structure of Businesses

Private sector businesses can be owned by individuals or groups of people.
These two pages are for AQA, OCR and Edexcel.

Sole Trader Businesses *are run by an* Individual

1) A sole trader is an **individual** trading in his or her own name, or under a suitable trading name. Sole traders tend to be **self-employed**, for example as shopkeepers, plumbers, electricians, hairdressers or consultants.

2) The essential feature of this type of business is that the sole trader has **full responsibility** for the **financial control** of his or her own business and for meeting **running costs** and **capital requirements**. The sole trader is fully responsible for all the **debts** of the business. This is called **unlimited liability**.

3) There are **minimal legal formalities** — the trader simply has to start trading. However, if the business isn't run under the proprietor's name, the trader needs to **register** the business name under the Business Names Act (1985).

'Capital' just means 'money'. 'Capital requirement' is money invested to set up a business or fund growth.

4) There are several **advantages** of being a sole trader:

- **Freedom** — the sole trader is their **own boss** and they have complete **control** over decisions.
- **Profit** — the sole trader is entitled to **all the profit** made by the business.
- **Simplicity** — there's **less form-filling** than for a limited company. Book-keeping is less complex.
- **Savings on fees** — there aren't any legal costs like you'd get with drawing up a partnership agreement or limited company documentation.

5) There are **disadvantages** too:

- **Risk** — there's **no one** to **share the responsibilities** of running the business with.
- **Time** — sole traders often need to **work long hours** to meet tight deadlines.
- **Expertise** — the sole trader may have **limited skills** in areas such as finance.
- **Vulnerability** — there's **no cover** if the trader **gets ill** and can't work.
- **Unlimited liability** — the sole trader is **responsible** for all the debts of the business.

A Partnership *is a* Group *of* Individuals *working together*

1) Examples of partnerships include groups of doctors, dentists, accountants and solicitors.

2) The law allows a partnership to have between **two** and **twenty partners**, although some **professions**, e.g. accountants and solicitors, are allowed **more** than twenty.

3) A partnership can either trade in the **names** of the partners, or under a suitable **trading name**.

4) Partnerships need rules. Most partnerships operate according to the terms of a **Partnership Agreement** (also called a **Deed of Partnership**). This is a document drawn up by a **solicitor** which sets out:

- The amount of capital contributed by each partner.
- The procedure in case of partnership disputes.
- How the profit will be shared between partners.
- Partners' voting rights.
- The procedures for bringing in new partners and old partners retiring.

There are **advantages** to a partnership:

1) More owners bring **more capital** to invest at start-up.
2) Partners can bring **more ideas** and **expertise** to a partnership.
3) Partners can **cover** for each others' **holidays** and **illness**.

There are **disadvantages** to a partnership:

1) Partners still have **unlimited liability**.
2) Each partner is liable for **decisions** made by **other partners** — even if they had **no say** in the decision.
3) There's a **risk** of **conflict** between partners.

Legal Structure of Businesses

Mutuals and Cooperatives are Owned by their Members

1) **Production cooperatives** are owned by their workers. All workers put money into the business and make business decisions.

2) **Retail cooperatives** are owned and controlled by their **customers**.

3) **Mutuals** are businesses which are owned by their **members**. **Building societies** are usually mutuals. Mutuals try to serve the interest of their members by providing a **good service**, rather than by trying to make **large** profits.

Liability to pay off Business Debts can be Limited or Unlimited

Sole traders and partnerships have unlimited liability

1) The **business** and the **owner** are **seen as one** under the **law**.

2) This means **business debts** become the **personal debts** of the owner. Sole traders and partners can be forced to **sell personal assets** like their **house** to pay off business debts.

3) Unlimited liability is a **huge financial risk** — it's an important factor to consider when deciding on the type of ownership for a new business.

Limited liability is a much smaller risk

1) Limited liability means that the owners **aren't personally responsible** for the debts of the business.

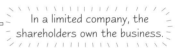
In a limited company, the shareholders own the business.

2) The **shareholders** of both **private** and **public limited companies** (see p.6) have limited liability, because a limited company has a **separate legal identity** from its owners.

3) The **most** the shareholders in a limited company can lose is the money they have **invested** in the company.

Some Partners in a partnership can have Limited Liability

1) The Limited Partnership Act 1907 allows a **partnership** to claim **limited liability** for **some** of its partners.

2) The partners with limited liability are called **sleeping partners**.

3) Sleeping partners can put **money** into the partnership but they **aren't allowed** to do anything to **run** the business.

4) There must be at least one **general partner** who **is fully liable** for all **debts** and obligations of the partnership.

Practice Questions

Q1   What legal requirements does a sole trader have to fulfil before he or she can start trading?

Q2   What's the maximum number of partners allowed in a dental practice?

Q3   What's the difference between limited liability and unlimited liability?

Q4   Which represents the biggest risk to the owners of a business — limited liability or unlimited liability?

Exam Question

Q1   Eric, a plumber trading as a sole trader, wants to go into partnership with his friend Sandra (also a plumber). What reasons might he have for wanting to change the type of ownership of his business? Advise him on the implications of doing so.

(6 marks)

Limited liability — it's a weight off your shoulders...

The difference between limited liability and unlimited liability is really important. Say someone puts £1500 into their own business. The business hits bad times, and eventually goes down the tubes owing £20 000. If the owner is a sole trader, he or she is liable to pay the full whack. If they're a shareholder of a limited company, they only lose the £1500 they put in.

Legal Structure of Businesses

Companies are different from partnerships. They're incorporated, which means they're a separate legal entity from the people who work in them. Companies are owned by shareholders. **This page is for AQA, OCR and Edexcel.**

There are two kinds of Limited Liability Companies — Ltds and PLCs

1) There are **private limited companies** and **public limited companies**.
2) Public and private limited companies have **limited liability** (see p.5).
3) They're owned by **shareholders** and run by **directors**.
4) Both require a minimum of only two shareholders, and there's no upper limit on the number of shareholders.

Private Limited Companies	Public Limited Companies
Can't sell shares to the public. People in the company own all the shares.	Can sell shares to the **public**. They must issue a **prospectus** to inform people about the company before they buy.
Don't have share prices quoted on **stock exchanges**.	Their share prices can be **quoted on the stock exchange**.
Shareholders may not be able to sell their shares without the **agreement** of the **other shareholders**.	Shares are **freely transferable** and can be bought and sold through stockbrokers, banks and share shops.
They're often **small** family businesses.	They usually start as private companies and then **go public later** to raise more capital.
There's **no minimum share capital** requirement.	They need **over £50 000** of share capital, and if they're listed on a stock exchange, **at least 25%** of this must be publicly available. People in the company can own the rest of the shares.
They end their name with the word "limited" or **Ltd**.	They always end their name with the initials **PLC**.

Companies are governed by the Companies Act (1985)

The Companies Act (1985) says that two important documents must be drawn up **before** a company can start trading. These are the **Memorandum of Association** and the **Articles of Association**.

1) The **Memorandum of Association** gives the company name followed by **Ltd**, if it's a private limited company, or **PLC**, if it's a public limited company, and it gives the company's business address.
2) The Memorandum of Association says what the **objectives** of the company are.
3) It gives **details** of the company's capital, e.g. £250 000 divided into 250 000 Ordinary Shares of £1 each.
4) It states clearly that the **shareholders' liability is limited**.

1) The **Articles of Association** are the **internal rules** of the company.
2) They give the **names** of the **directors**.
3) They say **how directors are appointed** and what kind of **power** they have.
4) The Articles of Association say what the **shareholders' voting rights** are.
5) They set out when and how the company will hold **shareholders meetings**.
6) The Articles of Association set out how the company will **share its profits**.

Companies House is where records of all UK companies are kept.

The **Memorandum of Association** and **Articles of Association** must both be sent to **Companies House**.
The Registrar of Companies issues a **Certificate of Incorporation** so that the company can start trading.
Once it's up and running, the company is legally obliged to produce **Annual Reports** of its financial activities.

Companies are controlled by Shareholders and Directors

1) All the shareholders in a **small** private limited company are usually the **directors**. The shareholders who hold the **most shares** have the **most power**.
2) In larger private limited companies, directors are **elected** to the board by **shareholders**. The board makes the important decisions. **Shareholders vote** on the performance of the board at the Annual General Meeting (**AGM**).
3) Shares in a PLC can be owned by **anyone**. The people who **own** the company (the shareholders) don't necessarily **control** the company. This is called "**divorce of ownership and control**".

Legal Structure of Businesses

Franchises are **Special Agreements** between **One Business** and **Another**

1) Franchises aren't really a type of business ownership as such. They're **agreements** (contracts) which allow one business to use the **business idea**, **name** and **reputation** of another business.

2) The **franchisor** is the business which is willing to sell, or license, the use of its idea, name and reputation. The **franchisee** is the business which wants to use the name.

3) Several well-known retail chains in the UK operate as franchises, e.g. KFC, Burger King, McDonald's, Prontaprint, Pizza Hut and The Body Shop.

The franchise contract gives franchisees these benefits:

1) A **well known name**.
2) A **successful** and **proven** business idea.
3) **Training** and **financial support** to set up a new franchise outlet.
4) **Marketing, advertising** and **promotion** are done **nationally** by the franchisor.
5) **Buying** is done **centrally** by the franchisor — this helps outlets keep **costs** down.
6) Expensive equipment can be **leased** from the franchisor.

The franchise contract gives franchisors these benefits:

1) Someone else to **run bits of their business** for them.
2) They **get paid** for the **use of their name**, and they get a **share of the profits**.
3) The more franchises there are, the faster the **name of the business** can be **spread**.
4) The **risk** involved in opening an outlet in a new location is **reduced**.

Mmmmm...sweet juicy franchise burgers

A franchisee has these responsibilities to the franchisor:

1) They have to **pay** the franchisor for the right to use the name.
2) They have to pay the franchisor part of the **profits**.
3) They have to run the business according to the franchisor's **rules**.
4) They have to **add value** to the franchisor's business concept by **working hard** and giving **good customer service**.

A franchisor has these responsibilities to the franchisee:

1) They have to **help** the franchisee set up a new franchise.
2) They provide a **good business concept** in the first place.

Practice Questions

Q1 What's the difference between the Memorandum of Association and the Articles of Association of a company?
Q2 State who holds power and influence in: a) a small private limited company, b) a large PLC.
Q3 What's meant by the term "divorce of ownership and control"?
Q4 Identify five differences between a Ltd company and a PLC.
Q5 Give two benefits of running a business as a franchise.

Exam Question

Q1 Describe the advantages and disadvantages of franchising, for both the franchisor and the franchisee. (4 marks)

<u>Keep good company — check your articles of association...</u>

Blimey — there are a lot of different ways of owning a business. Be careful you don't refer to all businesses as "companies". A limited company is different to a sole trader or partnership because it exists as a separate legal, uh, "thing" to the people who own and run the business, and it's set up using special legal documents.

Classification of Businesses

You can classify businesses by size, geography, economic sector and type of ownership.
These two pages are for OCR and Edexcel.

Businesses can be Classified by Size

There are different ways to measure the size of a business.

(1) **Number of Employees**

The Department of Trade and Industry (DTI) uses these classifications:

- 0-9 employees — a **micro business**
- 0-49 employees — a **small business** (includes micro businesses)
- 50-249 employees — a **medium-sized business**
- over 250 employees — a **large business**

In practice, it can actually be quite difficult to measure the size of a business. A company might only employ 40 people but its turnover could be well over £10 million. According to the number of employees the DTI would classify it as a small business but the turnover suggests it's much larger.

(2) **Turnover**

Size can also be measured by the **sales revenue** that a business earns. For example, a business with an annual turnover of £5500 million would be classified as a **large** business regardless of the number of employees.

(3) **Profit**

For example, a business with a pre-tax profit of £400 million would be considered **larger** than a business that made a pre-tax profit of £20 million.

Measuring size by profits can be misleading — profits go down when a business hits problems. A large business in difficulties wouldn't have great profits.

(4) **Asset value**

This is the **value** of the things (e.g. buildings and equipment), and **money** the business owns and any **stock** and **debtors** it may have. A business with an asset value of £750 million is obviously larger than a business with an asset value of only £70 million.

(5) **Market share**

Market share (see p.2) can be used to determine a firm's size in terms of the **market** it operates in. For example, a firm with a market share of 40% can be called larger than one with a more modest 10% share of the market.

(6) **Size relative to other businesses in the same industry**

You can compare businesses in the same industry, based on all the above criteria — number of employees, turnover, profit, asset value and market share. Depending on the **industry**, **some criteria** might be **more important** than others.

Businesses can be classified by Geography

1) Businesses can be local, regional, national or multinational.

2) A **multinational** business owns or controls production / service **facilities** in **different countries**. Multinationals don't just export their products to different countries — their business is **based** in different countries.

3) Small and medium-sized businesses are most likely to operate **locally** or **regionally**.

4) Large businesses are far more likely to operate on a **national** or **multinational** level.

Classification of Businesses

Businesses can be Classified by Economic Sector

You can also classify businesses according to what **stage** of the **production process** the business is involved in. There are three divisions — **primary**, **secondary** and **tertiary**.

Primary Sector

This sector covers the **farming**, **fishing** and **mining** industries. These are industries that **extract raw materials** from natural resources.

Primary sector industries are in decline in the UK. The UK economy is now mainly tertiary sector.

Secondary Sector

The secondary sector **processes** the raw materials that come from the primary sector. Secondary industry includes **manufacturing** (e.g. cars, tinned food, steel) and **construction** (e.g. building houses, factories, roads).

Tertiary Sector

This is the **service sector** which trades with businesses in the primary and secondary sectors and so helps them to sell their goods. It also includes some direct services to individuals. Examples include shops, banks, insurance companies, restaurants, hotels, and healthcare services.

Businesses are Classified by Type of Ownership

Private sector businesses are owned by individuals or groups of individuals

Most UK businesses are private sector. The objective of private sector businesses is to make **profit** for the owners. The private sector includes sole traders, partnerships, private limited companies, public limited companies, cooperatives and franchises.

> The UK economy is called a mixed economy because it's got public sector and private sector organisations.

Public sector businesses and organisations are owned or controlled by the government

The main objective of public sector organisations is to provide a **service** to the public. Examples include central and local **government services** like schools and street cleaning, **public corporations** like the NHS and **quangos** (government-funded committees) like the Arts Council are **public sector** organisations.

> Quasi-autonomous non-governmental organisation. Phew ... stick to quango.

The voluntary sector includes not-for-profit organisations, e.g. charities and charitable trusts

Charities are **independent** bodies run by full-time professionals and supported by **volunteers** — e.g. Oxfam, Shelter and the NSPCC. **Charitable trusts** operate as businesses but **pay less tax than ordinary businesses**. Examples of charitable trusts include independent schools and the National Trust.

Practice Questions

Q1   Summarise the main ways of classifying a business.
Q2   Why might you choose not to classify the size of a business by the number of employees?
Q3   Give an example of: a) a primary sector business, b) a public sector business, c) a multinational business.

Exam Question

Q1   Describe the different ways of measuring the size of businesses and discuss how useful they are for comparing firms in the same industry.
(9 marks)

I always thought a quango was a kind of extinct horse. Or a duck...

When someone says a business is "small" or "large" it isn't always obvious what they mean. A business can have a large turnover, but not make a huge profit. A business can have a small number of employees, but a massive share of the market. The primary / secondary / tertiary sectors are more clear-cut.

Marketing and Market Analysis

Marketing is "the management process responsible for identifying, anticipating and satisfying consumer requirements profitably." Well, that's what the Chartered Institute of Marketing says — I suppose they'd know. **For AQA, Edexcel, OCR.**

Marketing identifies customer Needs and Wants

1) Marketing finds out what customers **need and want**. Marketing also tries to **anticipate** what they'll want in the future so that businesses can get **one step ahead** of the market.

2) Marketing tries to ensure that the business supplies **goods and services** that customers **want** in order to **make profit**. It's mutually beneficial — the customer gets something they like, the business makes a profit.

3) Marketing covers **research**, **analysis**, **planning** and the "**marketing mix**". The "marketing mix" is all the decisions a business makes about promoting and selling a product.

4) Most larger businesses have a specialised **marketing department** — but marketing affects all departments.

Marketing is a Continual Process

Businesses start by deciding on **marketing objectives** — figuring out what they want to **achieve** in terms of **sales**.

1) Businesses **plan marketing strategies** to achieve their objectives. They **decide** which marketing **activities** to do, based on their **research** and **analysis**.

2) They put their **strategies** into **action** and carry out **marketing activities**.

3) They **monitor sales** to make sure their marketing strategies are having the **right effect**.

4) They **change and improve** their marketing **strategies** and **activities** — if they **need** to.

Markets are where Sales Happen — they aren't Limited to a Physical Place

Traditionally the term "**market**" meant the physical **place** where people traded their goods. Today the term includes **websites** like eBay, the **global market** for commodities, e.g. for oil or coffee and **financial markets** such as the London Stock Exchange.

"Market" also describes the **type** of **product or service** being bought and sold — the leisure market, the computer hardware market, the global oil market etc.

1) **Niche Markets** serve **specialist consumers**. They can give **high profit margins** — i.e. there can be a big **difference** between what it **costs** to make something and what the business can **sell** it for.

2) **Mass markets** sell ordinary things to very large numbers of people at quite cheap prices. Businesses can get **high volume sales** but at a fairly **low profit margin**. (There's more about niche and mass markets on p.19).

3) **Industrial markets** are where businesses sell products and services to other businesses, such as wholesalers supplying retailers. They are sometimes referred to as "**business to business**" markets or "**B2B**".

4) **Consumer markets** are where firms sell to individual customers — e.g. high street shops like Currys and Next. These markets are sometimes referred to as "business to consumer" or "**B2C**".

Marketing approaches can be Product, Market or Asset Oriented

1) **Product oriented** businesses start by deciding what they can **produce**. They put the **product** ahead of **customer needs** or **budget** constraints.

2) It's a **risky** strategy, because customers might want or need a **different product** altogether.

1) **Market oriented** or **customer oriented** businesses start by finding out what the **customer wants**.

2) A **market oriented** approach is more likely to **succeed** than a product oriented approach.

1) **Asset-led marketing** combines **consumer wants** with the **strengths** (assets) of the business.

2) For example, when developing the **new Mini**, **BMW** linked the **market desire** for a new small car with their **reputation** for reliability and engineering expertise. Customers were happy to pay a **premium price**.

3) **Asset-led marketing** is now seen as the best route to long term **customer satisfaction** and **brand loyalty**.

OCR and Edexcel

OCR and Edexcel   OCR and Edexcel

Marketing and Market Analysis

Market Analysis tells a Business about the Market they're in

Market analysis lets businesses spot **opportunities** in a market by looking at **market conditions**. The most important conditions are **market size**, **growth** in the market and **market share**.

The more a firm understands about their market, the more likely they are to make good marketing decisions.

MARKET SIZE — by volume and by value

Businesses estimate the size of their market in terms of the **total number of sales** (volume of sales) or in terms of the **value** in pounds of **all the sales** in the market.

Market size and share have to be considered together. 10% of a £1m market is worth £100k, while 25% of a £200k market is only worth £50k.

MARKET GROWTH

Businesses need to know if the market is **growing** or **shrinking**. Competition is fierce in a shrinking market — there are fewer customers to go around. In a **growing** market, **several** firms can **grow easily**. Businesses may want to get out of a market that's getting smaller.

MARKET SHARE — sales as a percentage of total market size

Businesses like to know what **share** of the market they have. If **1 out of every 4** PCs bought was a Dell, this would mean that Dell had a **25% market share** (in terms of units sold). If **£1 out of every £10** spent on perfume was spent on Chanel, this would mean Chanel had a **10% market share** (in terms of sales value).

Market share = sales ÷ total market size × 100%

As well as size, share and growth, market analysis measures things like **profitability** and the **costs** of buying equipment and training staff so you can **get into** the market (entry costs).

Markets are Segmented into groups of Similar Customers

Different groups of customers have different needs. **Analysing** different parts (**segments**) of a market allows a business to **focus** on the needs of **specific groups** within a target market. Segmentation can be done by:

1) **Income**, e.g. luxury products are aimed at high income groups.
2) **Socio-economic class**, e.g. businesses can segment their market based on the kind of jobs people have — from senior professionals to unemployed people.
3) **Age**, e.g. businesses often target products at specific age groups — teens, pre-teens, 25-35 year olds etc.
4) **Gender**, e.g. chocolate manufacturers target some items at women (e.g. Flake) and some at men (e.g. Yorkie).
5) **Geographical region**, e.g. some products have a regional market — you don't often see laver bread outside Wales.
6) **Amount of use**, e.g. mobile phone suppliers market differently to heavy users and light users.
7) **Ethnic grouping**, e.g. new ethnic minority TV channels make it easier for businesses to target advertising at particular ethnic groups.

All the above methods focus on a **characteristic of the customer**. In addition, new segmentation methods categorise markets according to the **reasons** for buying a product — as an essential, to cheer yourself up, as a gift, etc.

Practice Questions

Q1 Describe the four stages of the marketing process, once marketing objectives have been decided.

Q2 What is the difference between product orientation and market orientation?

Q3 What is "market segmentation"?

Exam Questions

Q1 Imagine that high street fashion retailer Gap is planning to launch a range of compilation CDs. How would you advise them to develop this new type of product using an asset-led approach? (15 marks)

Q2 Outline how a retailer of women's clothing, such as Next, might segment their market. (6 marks)

Did you know — agoraphobia is literally "fear of the marketplace"...

...and although there are a lot of different kinds of market out there, you don't need to be frightened of any of them. Marketing's about knowing your market, knowing what people want, and knowing how to sell it to them. Asset-led marketing is the "in thing" in marketing because it lets a business match its strengths to customer wants. Smooth...

Market Research

Market research is the collection and analysis of market information such as customer likes and dislikes. It reduces the risk of mistakes, e.g. producing 6 million copies of an album of extended Cheeky Girls remixes. **For AQA, OCR and Edexcel**.

Market Research *is done for* Three Main Reasons

1) It helps businesses **spot opportunities**. Businesses research **customer buying patterns** to help them predict what people will be buying in the future. A business might use **research** to help them spot growing markets to get into — and declining markets to get out of. Research on customer likes and dislikes might show a gap in the market.

2) It helps them **work out what to do next**. Businesses research before launching a product or advertising campaign.

3) It helps them see if their **plans are working**. A business that keeps a keen eye on sales figures will notice if their marketing strategy is having the right effect.

> Market research can be **expensive**. **Bad market research** can lead to **disastrous business decisions**. Businesses need to **plan carefully** to make sure they get the **maximum benefit** from market research.

There's Quantitative *and* Qualitative *market research*

1) Quantitative research produces **numerical statistics** — facts and figures. It often uses multiple choice **questionnaires** that ask questions like: "When did you last buy this product? A: within the last day, B: within the last week, C: within the last month, D: within the last year, E: longer ago, F: have never bought this product." These are called **closed questions** because they have **fixed**, **predetermined** answers.

2) Qualitative research looks into the **feelings** and **motivations** of consumers. It uses **focus groups** that have in-depth discussions on a product, and asks questions like "How does this product make you feel?" These are called **open questions**. The **answer isn't restricted** to multiple choice options.

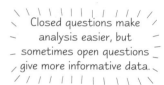
Closed questions make analysis easier, but sometimes open questions give more informative data.

There's Primary *and* Secondary *market research*

Primary market research is where a business **gathers new data** (or employs someone to do it on their behalf). **Secondary market research** is done by **analysing data** that's already available.

Primary *market research* — Find *the* Data Yourself

1) Primary data is gathered with **questionnaires**, **interviews**, post / phone / Internet **surveys**, **focus groups** and by observation (e.g. looking at CCTV to see how people shop in stores). Businesses do **test marketing** — they launch a product in one **region** and measure **sales** and **customer response** before launching it across the country.

2) Primary research uses **sampling** to make predictions about the **whole market** based on a sample.

3) Primary data is needed to find out what consumers think of a **new product** or **advert**. You can't use secondary data because, erm, there won't be any secondary data on a brand new product.

4) Primary data is **specific** to the purpose it's needed for. This is great for **niche markets** — secondary data might be too broad or too mainstream to tell you anything useful.

5) Primary data is **exclusive** to the business who commissioned the research, so **competitors can't benefit** from the research.

6) Primary research is always **up to date**.

7) **But**, primary research is **labour intensive**, **expensive** and **slow**.

Secondary *market research* — *the* Data's Already There

1) **Internal sources** of data include loyalty cards, feedback from company salesmen and analysis of company sales reports, financial accounts, and stock records.

2) **External sources** include government publications like the Social Trends report, marketing agency reports, pressure groups and trade magazines.

3) **Secondary data** is much **easier**, **faster** and **cheaper** to get hold of than primary data.

4) Secondary data that was gathered for a different purpose might be **unsuitable**. It may contain **errors** and it may be **out of date**.

5) Secondary data is often used to get an **initial understanding** of a market. A business may then do more specific primary research to investigate any **issues** or problems that are shown up by the secondary data.

Gretel and Bob liked to share a tender moment along with some secondary research data

Market Research

Market researchers need a Representative Sample

1) Market researchers can't ask the **whole** of a **market** to fill in a survey. They select a sample.

2) When they select the sample they try to make it **represent** the market. The sample must have **similar proportions** of people in terms of things like age, income, class, ethnicity and gender. If the sample isn't representative, you've got **problems**. However, it isn't always easy to get a representative sample.

3) A **big sample** has a better **chance** of being representative than a **small sample**. Even a big sample won't necessarily be 100% representative. There's always a **margin of error**.

Random sampling is where names are selected at random. It represents the **population as a whole**.

1) **Simple Random Sample** — Pick names **randomly** from a list (usually from the electoral register).

2) **Stratified Sample** — Divide the population into groups and make a **random selection** of people with the **right characteristics** (e.g. people old enough to have a driving licence).

3) **Systematic Sample** — Pick **one** name **randomly** from a list, then pick further names based on a **pattern** — e.g. every fourth name after the first one, or every tenth name after the first one.

Non-random sampling is... yup... when you don't pick the names at random.

1) **Quota Sample** — Pick people who fit into a **category** (say, 100 working mums between 30 and 40). Businesses use quota sampling to get opinions from the people the product is directly targeted at.

2) **Cluster Sample** — Pick respondents based on geographic area. It's suitable for products with a defined catchment area, e.g. a restaurant.

Market research needs to Avoid Bias

The quality of decisions made using market research is only as good as the **accuracy** of the research.

1) Researchers have to be careful and avoid any possible **bias**.

2) Questionnaires and interviews should avoid **leading questions**. These are questions that are phrased in a way that **leads** the respondent to give a particular answer. Leading questions should be weeded out when designing a questionnaire.

3) Interviews suffer from "**interviewer effects**". This is when the **response** isn't what the interviewee **really thinks**. This can be caused by the **personality** of the interviewer — their **opinions** can **influence** the interviewee.

4) Interviewers should only ask for personal data at the **end** of an interview so that they aren't influenced by knowing the **age** or **social background** of the interviewee.

5) The more **representative** a sample is, the more **confidence** a business can have in the results of the research.

Practice Questions

Q1 A toy company is researching the market for a new board game.
Write three open and three closed questions that they could use in a consumer survey.

Q2 List two internal and two external sources of secondary data.

Q3 Give three reasons why firms carry out market research.

Q4 What is the difference between quantitative secondary research and qualitative primary research?

Exam Question

Q1 Discuss why some businesses decide to pay market research companies to gather and help analyse data. (8 marks)

Surveys show that most people lie in surveys...

Research takes time and costs money — businesses must make sure the data's accurate or it'll be as much use as a chocolate fireguard. They also have to actually use the findings to provide what their customers want. If a business can use market research to increase their sales and profits, the market research will pay for itself. Everyone's a winner.

Statistics in Business

It's important to be able to understand market research statistics.
These pages are for AQA and Edexcel.

Market Research produces Statistics

1) Market research provides a lot of figures. These numbers have to be presented in a way that makes them **easy to understand**.

2) Results from primary research such as a questionnaire can be summarised in a **data logging sheet** — which tallies the number of responses to each option of each multiple choice question.

Question How often do you buy Supercola?	Number of respondents	% of total respondents
More than 5 times a week	1	5%
2-5 times a week	5	25%
1-2 times a week	8	40%
Between once a month and once a week	2	10%
1-10 times a year	1	5%
I never buy Supercola	3	15%
Total respondents	**20**	**100%**

Diagrams make Data Easier to Understand — and have High Visual Impact

1) **Pie charts** are used for showing **market share**. They can also show the proportions of different respondents within one sample. Each **1% share** is represented by a **3.6°** section of the pie (because there's 360° in a circle and 360 ÷ 100 = 3.6). Pie charts are **simple to use** and **easy** to **understand**. They can be quickly created with **spreadsheets**.

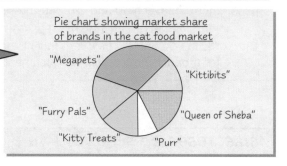

Pie chart showing market share of brands in the cat food market
"Megapets" "Kittibits" "Furry Pals" "Queen of Sheba" "Kitty Treats" "Purr"

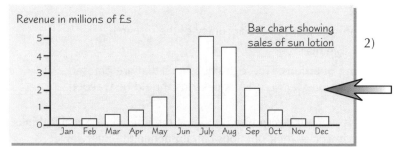

Revenue in millions of £s
Bar chart showing sales of sun lotion
Jan Feb Mar Apr May Jun July Aug Sep Oct Nov Dec

2) **Bar charts** show different values for a **single variable**. They're **easy** to **construct**, easy to **interpret** and they have **high visual impact**. The drawback is the potential for **confusion** if the **vertical scale** doesn't start at **zero** (it can look like there's a big difference between two bars, when there isn't really).

3) A **histogram** looks quite similar to a bar chart. However, in a histogram the **area** of the block is proportional to the value of the variable measured (not just the height). So a histogram is different from a bar chart because the bars can vary in both **width** and **height**. Histograms are suitable for comparing variables with **large ranges**.

4) A **pictogram** is a bar chart or histogram where the bars are **pictures** — logos or images. Pictograms are often used in **corporate brochures**, for instance Cadbury might use pictures of their choccie bars in their sales charts.

5) **Line graphs** plot one variable against another — e.g. sales against time. **More lines** can be added on to show **more variables** — they should be in different colours to keep the graph easy to read.

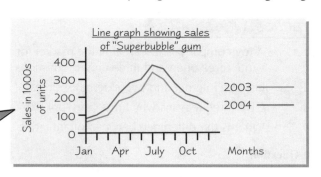

Line graph showing sales of "Superbubble" gum
Sales in 1000s of units
400 300 200 100 0
Jan Apr July Oct Months
2003 2004

It's Important to be able to Analyse Data and Graphs

As well as being able to read graphs and charts, you need to be able to **analyse** them. This means you need to be able to say what you think is the **important bit** of the chart — e.g. an upward trend, or a big market share. You need to be able to say what you think is causing it, and what the potential effects on marketing might be.

Statistics in Business

Data is clustered around an Average — Mean, Median or Mode

1) The **mean** is found by **adding together** all numbers in a data set and **dividing** the total by the **number of values** in the data set. Shops often calculate the mean spend per customer as the starting point of a marketing campaign aimed at increasing customers' spending per shop visit.

Example: 10 customers spend £5.90, £27.98, £13.62, £24.95, £78.81, £16.99, £13.20, £9.95, £2.58 and £14.96.

$$\text{Mean spend} = \frac{5.9 + 27.98 + 13.62 + 24.95 + 78.81 + 16.99 + 13.20 + 9.95 + 2.58 + 14.96}{10} = \frac{208.94}{10} = 20.89$$

2) The **median** is the **middle** value in a data set — once all the values are put in **ascending order**. A business might rank all salespeople by the revenue they've generated over the past month, then identify the **median** and pay everyone above this position a bonus for good performance.

Example: 15 sales people generate revenue of £1200, £1350, £1400, £1500, £1600, £1750, £1900, £1950, £2100, £2200, £2340, £2400, £2450, £2500, £2950.

Median sales revenue = the middle number, which is the 8th number = £1950

3) The **mode** is the **most common number** in a data set. Marks & Spencer might check the modal dress size when planning their shop displays so that the mannequins would reflect the most common body size among British women.

Example: 15 women have the following dress sizes: 10, 12, 16, 14, 12, 14, 8, 18, 16, 14, 12, 14, 10, 14, 16.

Modal dress size = 14

The Range of Data is Important as well

1) Averages can be a bit misleading. The **mean** of a **small range** of values is likely to give a **true picture** of the data. The **mean** of a **large** range of values can be misleading. It'd give a number somewhere in the middle of the range, and this wouldn't show that some of the values were actually really big or really small.

2) A **standard deviation** is a number which shows the **spread** or **range** of a set of values around the average. You don't have to know how to work out a standard deviation. All you need to know is that a **large** standard deviation means the numbers in the original data set are **spread out** a lot, and a **small** standard deviation means they're **clumped close together**.

3) A **confidence level** is another statistical trick. It indicates how **accurate** the research is. A confidence level of 95% means managers can assume the prediction would be correct 19 times out of 20.

Practice Questions

Q1 Explain the difference between the "mean", "median" and "mode" of a set of data.

Q2 Define the term "confidence level".

Q3 Calculate the angle of a sector of a pie chart that represents a company with 15% market share.

Exam Questions

Q1 Discuss how statistics can hinder as well as help decision making. (10 marks)

Q2 Explain why statistics are often used in advertising. (9 marks)

There are lies, damned lies and statistics...

Statistics can be very helpful but they can also be biased. If you're given a table or graph as part of an exam question, watch out for things like: how the axes are labelled, whether the axes start at zero, whether important info is left out. Remember that businesses often use graphs and charts to put facts and figures in as good a light as possible.

Marketing and Strategy

Businesses have to have some kind of objective or goal to their marketing.
These pages are for AQA, OCR and Edexcel.

Strategy *and* Planning *are an important part of* Marketing

1) **Corporate objectives** are **long term business aims**. They define the goals that a business is trying to achieve.

2) Businesses develop **long term marketing objectives** from their overall corporate objectives. Marketing objectives give a **direction** to all the marketing that the business does. Marketing objectives always need to take into account what **competitors** are up to.

3) Once a business has sorted out its marketing objectives, it develops **medium term marketing strategies** as **action plans** to achieve the marketing objectives.

4) Next, they think up **short term tactics** to put these medium term plans into action. **Tactics** are **individual marketing actions**, e.g. buying advertising space in a magazine, doing a "3 for the price of 2" promotion.

> Remember, a **strategy** is a **plan** of how to **achieve an objective**.
> A **tactic** is an **activity** that you do to **fulfil your strategy** and get closer to your objective.

Marketing planning is particularly important for **market oriented businesses**. Market orientation means that the **customer** is the focus of **everything** the business does (see p.10). This makes the **marketing department** the key **link** between the customer and the business. It's the marketing department who think up ways of communicating with the customer, giving them good products, and making them happy.

Marketing Objectives *must be* Specific

Marketing objectives should be **measurable** and **time-specific** — e.g. "to increase sales of Brand A by 15% over two years". They should also be **realistic**. There's no point in aiming for the moon.

1) The simplest and most common marketing objective is to increase sales. Businesses can go for an objective of increasing sales volume (the number of units that they sell) or sales value (the amount of money they get from sales).

2) Increasing market share is another common objective. Large, well established businesses can set an objective of maintaining the market share they already have.

3) Businesses can set objectives to grow or develop particular markets. For example, they could set an objective of reaching £1 million worth of sales in the French beer market within two years of starting to export beer to France.

4) Businesses can go for an objective of improving customer satisfaction. This would be necessary if they'd recently got a bad rating in customer surveys.

5) Businesses with highly seasonal sales can set an objective of getting more sales in the rest of the year. For example, a Christmas cracker manufacturer could market crackers for parties all year round.

6) A firm might set the objective of increasing sales of its most profitable products.

Adding Value *is an important part of marketing* — *AQA and Edexcel*

Added value is the **difference** between the **cost** of producing the product and the actual **selling price** of the final product or service. Added value means added **profit**, so **marketing objectives** should aim to **add value** to a product or service. Marketing can add value to products through different strategies:

1) Having a **Unique Selling Point** (USP) for the product — a unique feature that other products don't have and which customers are willing to pay more for. The USP must **differentiate** the product from competitor products. Businesses have to be careful that rivals don't **copy** their USP.

2) Making a product or service **attractive** to customers through a mix of design, function, image and good customer service. For example, a manufacturer can charge a lot more for products in **pretty packaging** than the packaging costs to make. A supermarket website can charge more for its **home delivery service** than the actual cost of delivery.

3) **Branding** the product effectively. A good brand **suggests** good design, function, image and service. Brand names like "Nike" allow clothing manufacturers to charge **three or four times the price** they'd be able to charge for the same item without the logo — which proves that **branding adds value**.

AQA and Edexcel

Marketing and Strategy

Developing a Marketing Strategy is an Ongoing Process

1) First of all, a business has to set its **marketing objectives**.

2) Then, they need to identify the **major strengths** and **weaknesses** of the **business**. These are **internal factors** like brand value, employee skills, relationships with buyers and suppliers, technical knowledge, the state of manufacturing machinery, financial stability and distribution networks.

3) They also need to spot the main **opportunities** and **threats** in the **marketplace**. These are **external factors** — in particular things that **competitors** are doing, but also all the social, technological, economic, environmental and legal changes that affect the market.

4) The marketing strategy has to be the **best** way of reaching the **marketing objective** for that **particular business**. It has to play to the firm's **strengths**, try to fix any **weaknesses**, make the most of **opportunities** and fight off **threats**.

5) Businesses **review** the marketing strategy to **see if it's working**, and **change** it if it isn't.

6) They need to **update** the strategy if any important factors in the company or the market have changed.

7) Managers keep on checking the strategy all the time to see if it needs tweaking. A marketing strategy is **never completely finished**.

Investigating strengths, weaknesses, opportunities and threats is called SWOT analysis. There's more about it on p.86-87.

There are some examples of marketing strategies on p.18-19.

Marketing strategies can Respond to Internal and External Factors

1) A good marketing strategy should **link** the **strengths** of the business with **opportunities** in the market.

2) It **addresses weaknesses** in a business and tries to fix them. A marketing strategy can do this by **ditching problem products** or by **spending money** to **improve** them and get them making more profit. A marketing strategy can aim to fill gaps in a business's **product portfolio** by developing new products.

3) It reacts to **threats** such as competitor actions. It's really important to not get caught napping when your **major competitor** comes out with a new product, or a new ad campaign — or cuts the price of their brand. Businesses need to re-emphasise the benefits of their brand to fight back against their competitors.

4) As well as competitor actions, other changes in the market can threaten a firm's position, and clever marketing is needed to cope with them. **Changes** in customer **needs** threaten sales — a business might react by coming up with new products, or sell existing products to new customers. **Advances in technology** can make existing products obsolete — businesses either have to come up with new products, or maybe cut the price of their old products and market them to the "cheap" end of the market.

Above all else, Marketing Strategies should Work

OK, it kind of goes without saying — but it is important. A good marketing strategy should **work**. It should get the business as **close** to its marketing objective as **possible**.

Practice Questions

Q1 Explain the difference between an objective, a strategy and a tactic.
Q2 State four common marketing objectives.
Q3 What's meant by "added value"?

Exam Questions

Q1 Explain the importance of USPs to the marketing of products. (4 marks)

Q2 Discuss what marketing objectives would be most suitable for a well established multinational airline. (10 marks)

So you don't just shove a price tag on it and stick it on the shelf, then...

There's a lot more thinking and planning to marketing than you might expect. After doing market research to find out what's going on in the market, managers then have to work out exactly what they want to achieve with a product, and exactly how they're going to achieve it. And they keep checking to make sure it's right. A marketing manager's work is never done...

Marketing and Strategy

These pages are for AQA. *The terms you need to get your head around are market penetration, product development, market development, diversification, mass marketing and niche marketing.*

There are **Four** main kinds of **Market Strategy** — with **Different Risks**

1) **Market penetration** means trying to sell more products to an existing market. A business can do this by increasing its **market share** — taking customers away from its competitors. It can also sell more to its existing market when the whole market grows — all businesses in the market get more sales.

2) **Mobile phone providers** have a **market penetration** strategy. They're growing in size because the whole mobile phone market is still growing. They're also trying to increase their share of the market at the expense of other mobile phone providers.

3) **Market penetration** is a great strategy for growth. It isn't very **risky**. Selling more of the **same** product to people you already have a **relationship** with is relatively **simple**.

1) **New product development** means developing **new** products to sell to existing customers. The new product can be a **replacement** of an old product, or something **completely new**.

2) Sony followed a **new product development** strategy when they introduced the Walkman, and again when they developed the Discman to replace the Walkman.

3) **New product development** is slightly riskier. A business can use an **existing relationship** with its customers to get them to buy new things, but they have to make sure that the **product is right**.

1) **Market development** is when a business finds a **new market** for its **existing products**. This can be a new segment of the market, or a new geographical area.

2) Johnson & Johnson followed a **market development** strategy when they marketed their baby powder and baby oil for use by **adults** as talcum powder and skin moisturiser. Fewer people were using baby powder on actual babies, so Johnson and Johnson needed a new marketing strategy.

3) **Market development** is a little more **risky** because it's harder to get **new people** to start buying than it is to sell new things to existing customers.

1) **Diversification** is when a business develops **new products** or **services** to sell in a market that it **doesn't** already operate in. Businesses can also diversify by **buying another business** that operates in a different market.

2) JCB and Caterpillar are manufacturers of **construction equipment**. They both decided to go into the **men's clothing market** — making chunky work-style boots, belts and hats featuring the company logo.

3) **Diversification** is a **high risk strategy**. A business going for diversification needs to develop a **great new product** and find out about a **new market** at the **same time**, which is difficult. Businesses trying to diversify don't have experience in their new market, and could end up making mistakes.

4) Businesses need a **strong brand name** to diversify successfully.

Marketing Strategies must match **Business Characteristics**

Businesses have to decide whether they have the **resources** for a potential marketing strategy before they **commit** to it.

1) **Small** businesses need **modest** strategies that won't break the bank. Big **multinational** corporations usually have **several objectives** with each one backed up by a whole **load of strategies**.

2) **Market leaders** are most likely to have marketing strategies that try to **keep** them at the **top of the market**. **Smaller** firms need strategies that try to keep them **surviving** in the market.

3) Highly **competitive** markets need **good strategies**. No shock, Sherlock.

4) Businesses can make use of strengths like a good brand name or a good distribution network. A business with a strong **brand name** may decide to **diversify** and use its brand in new markets. A business with a good **network of retail outlets** could try selling a **larger range of products** in its shops.

5) New **opportunities** for making, selling or advertising need **new strategies** to make the **most** of them.

Marketing and Strategy

Mass Marketing is selling Large Quantities of Standardised Goods

1) A **mass market** is a large market containing **lots of customers** with **similar requirements**.

2) Businesses in a mass market sell **standardised goods** at **cheap prices** to **lots of customers**. Mass market goods include things like washing machines, TVs, teabags, and tins of beans.

3) **Mass production techniques** developed in the 19th and 20th centuries, e.g. assembly line production, made a mass market possible. These techniques meant that production could be large scale and cost effective — producing **standardised** goods at **low prices**.

4) **Globalisation** is the process where goods and consumer desires become standardised across international borders. Globalisation has **increased the size** of the **mass market** and made **mass marketing** more **important**. You can sell Coca Cola anywhere on the planet.

5) In a mass market, businesses can grow big and benefit from productive **economies of scale** (see p.68) — but they must take care that they don't end up with **diseconomies** of scale (see p.69).

6) Mass marketing needs a **lot of resources**, e.g. lots of machines and lots of workers. If **demand doesn't meet expectations**, machines and workers won't have enough to do — a **waste** of resources and money.

Product Differentiation is Important in a Mass Market

1) Businesses in a **mass market** need to use **marketing** to **differentiate** their product from all the other products on the market.

2) Even if the product **isn't actually all that different** from the others (e.g. a tin of baked beans or a bottle of washing up liquid), it's important that customers **see** it as **different** in some way — and somehow more **suited** to them.

Niche Marketing is selling to Small Segments of a market

1) Niche marketing picks out relatively **small market segments** and tries to cater **specifically** to them.

2) Niche marketing lets **small** firms survive. Small firms can offer **unique selling points** which appeal to a **small niche customer base** that larger firms simply wouldn't bother with.

3) Small niche **markets** suit small niche **manufacturers**. A small manufacturer can **meet the demand** of a **small segment** of the market. It might not be able to meet the demand of a **mass market**.

4) Another **benefit** of niche marketing is that a business can have **loyal customers** — who are often willing to pay **premium prices** for a product that's just right for them.

5) There's almost no potential to **grow** in a niche market. Niche businesses can't save costs by producing on a large scale — small scale manufacturers can't get bulk discounts from suppliers.

6) If **bigger firms** enter the market, niche manufacturers can **struggle to survive**. Bigger firms have lower costs and they can be more competitive.

Practice Questions

Q1 How can the size of a business affect its marketing strategy?

Q2 Explain what's meant by diversification and give examples.

Q3 Define the terms niche marketing and mass marketing.

Q4 Give two benefits of niche marketing for a small business.

Exam Questions

Q1 Analyse the importance of a strong brand image for a firm deciding on a new marketing strategy. (9 marks)

Q2 Jatinder works in the fashion industry. He wants to set up his own fashion label, focusing on a niche market of urban Asian youth. Discuss the advantages and disadvantages of choosing a niche marketing strategy. (10 marks)

Assess the "stay in bed" strategy for exam success...

Can you list those six terms that you're supposed to have in your head? If the answer is yes, then that's a good start. Unfortunately there's more to it than just listing them — in the exam you can be asked to evaluate a strategy and say how well it suits a particular business. This means you need to give pros and cons, and weigh up the arguments for both sides.

The Marketing Mix

The marketing mix is an odd term — it means all the things that can affect a decision to buy something, or leave it on the shelf. **These two pages are for OCR, AQA and Edexcel.**

The **Marketing Mix** is the Four Ps — **Price**, **Product**, **Place** and **Promotion**

The marketing mix is the combination of factors that **affect a customer's decision to buy**. The **price** has to be right, the **product** has to be right, the product must be **distributed** to the right places, and it has to be **promoted** in the right way.

The factors in the marketing mix have to **work together**. Businesses may have to **compromise** on some elements — the budget for a product might not allow top dollar spending on **all** elements of the mix.

1) The **marketing mix** puts the marketing strategy into **practice**.
2) For example, a marketing strategy of **competition** with a low-priced competitor in a **mass market** means the product must be priced **cheaply**, which means it needs to be fairly **basic**. It'll need to be **widely** distributed.
3) The marketing mix has to **fit in** with other parts of the business. A business can only offer low prices if it can **afford** to. A business with a **poor distribution network** can't put widespread and fast distribution in its mix.

Different markets have a different **Marketing Mix**

Industrial markets	Consumer markets
One business supplies another with **raw materials**, **capital goods** (e.g. machines and buildings) or **services** (e.g. banking and security).	Businesses supply the **end user** with all kinds of products and services.
Businesses have a **few** customers.	Businesses have **many customers**.
There's a **close relationship** between buyer and seller.	There's a **remote relationship** between buyer and seller.
Distribution is **direct** from manufacturer to consumer.	**Distribution** goes through **warehouses** and **retail** shops.
Buyers tend to make **rational decisions** based on **price**, **quality** and **supply**. Packaging and advertising aren't so important.	**Branding**, **packaging** and **advertising** are **important**, as well as price, quality and supply.
Advertising is in **specialist media**.	Businesses advertise in **mass media**.
There are **flexible** terms of supply — salespeople can offer **special discounts** and **personal deals**.	Terms of supply are **fixed** — the customer pays the price that's on the price tag.

The **Product** is the most **Important** thing in the **Marketing Mix**

1) **Products** are whatever's being sold — like **goods** and **services**.
2) Marketing folk usually see the product as the most **important** ingredient of the marketing mix. A lousy product isn't likely to meet the needs of customers, even if the price, distribution and promotion are great.
3) Products give **tangible benefits** that can be measured — e.g. a washing powder that gets clothes clean, a car that gets good miles per gallon, a mortgage with a low interest rate and good terms and conditions.
4) Products also give **intangible benefits** that can't be measured — e.g. a treat that makes you feel good, a car with a reputation for good engineering that gives peace of mind, and street clothing with a good image that makes you feel all "cool" and stuff.
5) The **features** of a product are important — but so are things like **reliability**, **customer service**, money-back **guarantees** and how easy it is to get hold of **spare parts**.

Brands and Packaging are important
Edexcel

1) **Homogeneous** or **generic** products are the same no matter which business sells them. Brands are **unique**.
2) Brands are important because customers pay a **premium price** for them, and customers are **loyal** to them. Brands have a specific **brand image** — a good brand has a lot of **intangible benefits** for the customer.
3) Brands can be **individual** products — like Sprite or Daz or KitKat. They can also be "family brands" which cover a range of products, like Heinz or Nike.
4) Packaging is important because it helps to **distinguish** the product, e.g. the Coca-Cola bottle. Packaging also helps to give a good **image** of a product. Packaging isn't important for all products, e.g. those in industrial markets. A box of **fancy chocolates** needs attractive packaging, but a bulk order of **printer toner** doesn't.

Edexcel

The Marketing Mix

Price is part of the mix

1) Price determines the **revenue** that businesses get. Price is a **balance** between being **competitive** and being **profitable**. Too high, and people **won't buy**. Too low, and you won't make enough **profit**.

2) In a **competitive** market, customers have lots of **choice** — so price is an **important** factor. In a **monopoly**, there's only one seller in the market, and customers have no choice. A monopoly seller can charge **high** prices.

3) The price must **fit in** with the other aspects of the marketing mix, e.g. the quality and desirability of the product.

Businesses use different Pricing Methods

Cost-based pricing adds a bit onto the cost of production to come up with the selling price.

1) **Cost-plus pricing** takes direct and indirect costs of production into account, and adds a **fixed percentage** called the **mark-up**.

2) **Marginal pricing** or **contribution pricing** sets the price to be more than the **variable costs** per unit. The price of each unit makes a **contribution** to the **fixed costs**.

Market-oriented pricing is based on **demand** in the market.

1) **Penetration pricing** is when a product is given a low initial price to get into the market. As the volume of sales goes up, the price is increased. E.g. a magazine might start with a low price to get readers buying it.

2) **Price discrimination** is when different prices are charged for the same product — e.g. **plane tickets** vary in price depending on when you travel. Different groups of customers can be charged different prices.

3) **Skimming** or **creaming** means starting with a high price and reducing it later. The price can go down when the product has achieved economies of scale. **High tech** goods, e.g. video cameras and digital music players use this pricing strategy.

A product can keep a high price if it has strong brand values, a USP, or if it's seen as exclusive / luxury.

4) **Psychological pricing** bases the price on customers' **expectation** about what to pay. For example, a high price may make people think the product is high quality, and £99.99 seems better than £100 even though it's only 1p difference.

Competition-based pricing is based on the prices a competitor is charging.

1) Market leaders often act as **price maker**, or **price leader**. They set the price, and other businesses follow.

2) Competition reduces prices. In very competitive markets, **buyers dictate the price**, and sellers have to **take whatever price** the buyer is willing to pay — e.g. milk producers selling to supermarkets are **price takers**.

3) **Destroyer pricing** or **predatory pricing** is when a business **deliberately lowers prices** to force another business **out of the market** — e.g. **supermarket price wars**, when supermarkets cut the price of their own brand goods to very low levels. It's a **gamble** — the predatory business usually makes a **loss** on the product (products priced this way are known as **loss leaders**). They either need to be making enough profit on other products to **cover the loss**, or the rival business needs to go out of the market pretty quick so the **price can go up** again.

Practice Questions

Q1 What is the marketing mix?

Q2 Give examples of intangible benefits provided by a product.

Q3 What is cost-plus pricing?

Q4 What is destroyer pricing?

Exam Questions

Q1 Describe the methods a business might use to determine a price for its products. (6 marks)

Q2 How would the marketing mix be different for a product sold in an industrial market, compared to a product sold in a consumer market? (6 marks)

The Marketing Mix — just add water for perfect marketing...

With a general question on "the marketing mix" you need to cover product, price, promotion and place. But you can also get questions specifically about product, or about price. So, you really need to know your onions on price determination. If they ask you about price skimming, for example, you need to know what it is, and why a firm might use it.

The Marketing Mix: Promotion

These pages continue the fascinating tale of the marketing mix, and take you to the land of promotion — the land of ads in the back of Today's Golfer, three for the price of two, used car salesmen and direct mail. Glamorous, so 'tis. **These two pages are for all three exam boards — AQA, OCR and Edexcel.**

Promotion is part of the Marketing Mix

1) Promotion is designed either to **inform** customers about a product or service, or to **persuade** them to buy it (or both).

2) **Promotional objectives** include increasing **sales** and **profits** or increasing **awareness** of the product.

3) All promotion has to get the customer's **attention** so that they can be informed or persuaded about the product.

Above-the-Line Promotion is Advertising through the Media

1) Advertising is **non-personal communication** from a business to the public.

2) Ads are used to **promote goods and services** — and also to promote a firm's **public image**.

3) Advertising uses various **media** including print, film, TV, radio, billboards (also called hoardings) and the Internet. There are adverts on buses, on bus stops, on the pavement — almost **everywhere**.

4) The choice of media depends partly on the **number of target customers** and the number of **readers** or **viewers** who'll **see** the ad. Ideally, a business would want its adverts to be seen by as **much** of the target market as possible.

5) The **impact** of an ad is very important. A full page ad has more impact than a half page ad. It's important to put ads where people won't just see them, but **REALLY NOTICE THEM**.

The TV remote — scourge of TV advertisers everywhere. People are changing channel when the ads come on, the FIENDS....

6) Advertising **costs** a business **money**. The cost of an advertising campaign must be **worth it** in terms of the **extra sales** it creates. TV adverts at prime viewing times are very expensive. Ads shown when fewer people are watching are cheaper, but don't reach as many people.

7) **Specialist media** are used to advertise specialist products to **niche markets**. For example, a manufacturer of fish hooks would advertise in a monthly fishing magazine, not in the Telegraph newspaper.

8) **Mass media** are mainly used to advertise **mass market consumer** products and services. However, **business** equipment like computer systems, office paper and even computer file formats (e.g. PDF) are **advertised on TV** these days, so it's not right to say that mass media advertising is **only** for consumer products.

9) There are **legal constraints** on advertising some products. It's against the law to advertise spirits on billboards. **Cigarette** advertising in magazines and on billboards is also banned.

Advertising changes during a Product Life Cycle

See p.26-27 for more on product life cycles.

1) Products are often heavily advertised at **launch**. If a product is completely **new** to the market, the adverts are **informative**. They tell customers about the product.

2) During the **growth** phase, advertising **differentiates** between brands. It persuades consumers that the product is different from the competitors and better than the competitors. The objective of advertising in the growth phase is to **maintain** or **increase market share**.

3) When a product is at the **mature, saturation** phase, consumers need to be **reminded** of it. If the manufacturer has an **extension** strategy, they can use advertising to inform consumers about any **improvements** they've made to their product.

The Marketing Mix: Promotion

Below-the-Line promotion is Everything Else apart from advertising

1) **Sales promotions** are things like **special offers**, e.g. "buy one get one free" (BOGOF), competitions, free gifts, **point of sale displays** (e.g. special colourful racks with the company logo), **sponsorship**, and **trade-ins** (e.g. paying for part of a new car by giving the seller your old car). Sales promotions can be aimed straight at the **customer** to **raise awareness** or **increase sales** of a product. Manufacturers also do sales promotions aimed at the **retailer** to encourage them to **stock** more of their products.

2) **Direct mail** means **mailshots** sent out to customers. The customer usually hasn't **asked** to receive them. Businesses that keep information about their customers on a database can **target** their direct mail to particular consumer groups. Direct mail that is untargeted ("**junk mail**") can be a **waste of money**, because it often just gets thrown away. People can **resent** getting **too much** direct mail.

3) **Public relations** (**PR**) is a firm's attempt to put out a **good message** about itself and its products or services. PR includes **press releases** sent to the media and special **promotional events**.

4) **Personal selling** or **direct selling** is personal communication between a **salesperson** and a customer. Office equipment is often sold to businesses in this way. Personal selling includes sales assistants in shops as well as travelling salespeople and phone salespeople.

5) **Sponsorship** of **sports events** makes consumers aware of a firm and their product. It also gives the firm a good image.

Businesses use Lots of Promotional Methods

1) The combination of promotional techniques that a business uses to promote a product is called the **promotional mix**. The main elements in the mix are often **personal selling** and **advertising**. Other methods have a supporting role.

2) The promotional mix depends on: the **product** itself, the **market**, **competitor activity**, the **product life cycle** and the **budget** available.

3) In general, **inexpensive**, **simple** products purchased by the **consumer** are promoted by **advertising**.

4) **Expensive** and **complex** products are more likely to be promoted by **personal selling**. So are products or services sold in the **industrial market**.

5) **Consumer durables**, for example **cars** or **washing machines**, often use a combination of **advertising** and **personal selling**. TV, print and billboard adverts **attract the buyer** into the showroom, where the salesperson moves in for the kill.

6) Manufacturers use different methods to sell their product to a **retailer**, and to sell it to the **final customer**. Businesses often use **salespeople** to get **shops** to stock their product, and **advertising** to persuade **customers** to buy the product in the shops.

Practice Questions

Q1   What is "above-the-line" promotion?

Q2   In which phase of the product life cycle does advertising stress differences with competitor products?

Q3   Give two examples of "below-the-line" promotion.

Q4   What is the "promotional mix"?

Exam Questions

Q1   How might a business change its advertising according to a product's life cycle?   (4 marks)

Q2   How might a manufacturer of breakfast cereal use below-the line promotion to advertise their product?   (10 marks)

Above-the-line, below-the-line — I wonder where you draw the line...

One bit of exam advice — don't focus on advertising too much. Promotion includes special offers, point of sale displays, direct mail, etc. Each method of above-the-line promotion and below-the-line promotion has pros and cons in terms of cost, effectiveness and ability to reach different market segments. Promotion also has to suit the rest of the marketing mix.

The Marketing Mix: Distribution

Distribution is important. If a product can't get to the marketplace, no one can buy it. Needs go unfulfilled, companies don't make profits, anarchy reigns... **These two pages are for AQA, OCR and Edexcel.**

It's **Vital** to get the **Product** to the **Consumer**

A **channel** of **distribution** is the route a product takes from the producer to the consumer. A product usually passes through **intermediaries** on the way from producer to consumer — e.g. **retailers**, **wholesalers** and **agents**.

1) **Retailers** are **shops** who sell to consumers. They're usually the **final stage** in the distribution channel. Tesco, Argos and Amazon.co.uk are **retailers**. Retailers can be physical shops or online "e-tailers".

2) **Wholesalers** buy products cheaply in **bulk** and **sell them on** to **retailers**. Wholesalers make life **easier** for retailers and manufacturers:

   - Wholesalers **buy** goods from manufacturers as soon as they're produced. Wholesalers **store** the goods in bulk. This is called "**breaking bulk**" — the wholesaler takes the goods off the manufacturer's hands and **pays** for the whole lot. The manufacturer doesn't have to **wait** for the goods to be bought and paid for by customers before they see any cash.

   - Wholesalers make distribution **simpler**. Without a wholesaler, the manufacturer would have to make **separate deliveries** to lots of retailers, and send each and every retailer an **invoice**. Selling to one wholesaler cuts down the paperwork and the number of journeys.

   - Wholesalers can **store more goods** than a retailer can — they act as the retailer's storage cupboard.

3) **Agents** act on behalf of **manufacturers**.

There are **Different Channels** of **Distribution**

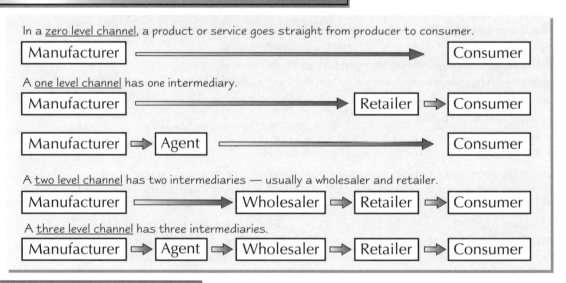

In a <u>zero level channel</u>, a product or service goes straight from producer to consumer.

| Manufacturer | ⟶ | Consumer |

A <u>one level channel</u> has one intermediary.

| Manufacturer | ⟶ | Retailer | ⇨ | Consumer |

| Manufacturer | ⇨ | Agent | ⟶ | Consumer |

A <u>two level channel</u> has two intermediaries — usually a wholesaler and retailer.

| Manufacturer | ⟹ | Wholesaler | ⇨ | Retailer | ⇨ | Consumer |

A <u>three level channel</u> has three intermediaries.

| Manufacturer | ⇨ | Agent | ⇨ | Wholesaler | ⇨ | Retailer | ⇨ | Consumer |

Direct Selling: Manufacturer – Consumer

Accountants, electricians and hairdressers sell their **services** direct to the consumer. The **Internet** has made it **easier** for producers of goods to sell **direct** to the consumer. Direct selling is also done through door-to-door sales, TV shopping channels, telephone sales and mail order catalogues.

Indirect Selling: Manufacturer – Wholesaler – Retailer – Consumer

This is the **traditional** distribution channel used for **fast moving consumer goods** (known as FMCG for short).

Indirect Selling: Manufacturer – Retailer – Consumer

Large supermarkets buy goods direct from the manufacturer and do their own wholesaling.

Direct Selling through an agent: Manufacturer – Agent– Consumer

Avon cosmetics and Ann Summers lingerie and sex toys are sold by **agents** through **party plans** — people invite friends to their **home** and an **agent** sells the goods **at the party**. Some **mail order catalogues** (e.g. Betterware) use agents who place orders on behalf of other people and collect payments from them.

The Marketing Mix: Distribution

Businesses choose a Channel of Distribution to Suit Their Business

The choice of distribution channel is a compromise between cost, ease and control.

1) It's **more profitable** to **sell direct** to the customer. Each intermediary in the distribution chain takes a **slice of profit** from the manufacturer — wholesalers and retailers have to make money too. Businesses that **sell direct** can offer their product at a **lower price** than **retailers** at the end of a long distribution chain.

2) On the other hand, it's **easier** to use **intermediaries**. It'd be a hassle to distribute a small amount of product to lots of little shops. It's easier to sell to a **wholesaler** who can deliver products from several manufacturers in a single batch delivery. Using a wholesaler gives a manufacturer the chance of more **market coverage**.

3) The **fewer intermediaries** in the distribution chain, the more **control** a manufacturer has over how its products are sold. They can decide the **final selling price** and how the product is **promoted**.

There are no real hard and fast rules about which distribution channel a business might choose, but there are a few trends.

Short Distribution Channels	Long Distribution Channels
Industrial products	Consumer products
Few customers	Many customers
Customers concentrated in one place	Customers widely spread out
Expensive, complex goods	Inexpensive, simple goods
Infrequent sales	Frequent sales
Bulky products	Small products
Bespoke (made to measure) products	Standard products
Services	Goods

Businesses set **distribution targets**. They might set a target of £X worth of sales through supermarkets, or selling to more retail outlets in a particular area of the country.

Different Distribution Strategies suit different products

1) **Everyday groceries** and **convenience** items need to be distributed as **widely** as possible. Consumers want to be able to buy things like a newspaper, a pint of milk and a bar of chocolate at a convenient local shop. They don't want to travel 20 miles to a "Pints Of Milk R Us" superstore.

2) **Luxury** goods don't need to be widely distributed. Manufacturers of luxury goods like to sell them in a small number of **exclusive** shops — it's about **quality**, not quantity.

3) Specialist goods like electrical products need to be distributed to **specialist** shops. Consumers like to be able to **compare** several different kinds of computer or CD player before buying, and often need specialist advice and assistance when selecting their purchase.

Practice Questions

Q1 What is the role of a wholesaler?
Q2 Name two types of channel of distribution.
Q3 What kind of distribution channel is traditionally used for FMCG?
Q4 What kind of distribution strategy is needed for everyday groceries?

Exam Questions

Q1 What factors must a business take into account when deciding on an appropriate channel of distribution for its products? (4 marks)

Q2 Evaluate Internet sales as a distribution channel for luxury consumer goods. (7 marks)

This page is dedicated to Long Distance Clara from Pigeon Street...

Distribution can seem like a mundane, boring thing. Yes, it is all about warehouses full of cardboard boxes, fleets of trucks going from A to B and funny little men popping the Betterware catalogue through your letterbox. But on the other hand it's a vital part of the wondrous marketing mix. Where you can buy something is a big factor in deciding whether to buy it.

Product Life Cycle

All products are born with no sales at all. If they're looked after, they grow into big strong products with lots of sales, then they get married and have lots of spin-offs ... er, maybe. **These two pages are for AQA, OCR and Edexcel.**

Products have a **Life Cycle**

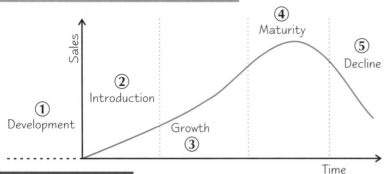

The product life cycle shows the **sales** of a product over **time**. It's useful for planning **marketing strategies** and changing the **marketing mix**.

1 — Development

1) The **research and development** (R&D) department **develop** the product.
2) The **marketing** department does **market research**.
3) The **costs** are **high**, and there aren't any sales yet to cover the costs.
4) Development has a **high failure rate**. This is because there's often **not enough demand**, or because the business can't make the product **cheaply** enough to make a profit.

2 — Introduction

1) The product is **launched**, either in one market or in several markets. It's sometimes launched with **complementary** products — e.g. the Playstation was launched with games.
2) The business often **promotes** the product heavily to build sales — but businesses need to make sure they've got enough **resources** and **capacity** to **meet the demand** that promotions create.
3) The **initial price** of the product may be **high** to cover **promotional costs**. This is **skimming** (see p.21).
4) Alternatively, the price can start off **low** to encourage sales. This is **penetration pricing** (see p.21).
5) Sales go up, but the sales revenue has to pay for the high **fixed cost** of development **before** the product can make a **profit**. The business ditches products with disappointing sales.
6) There aren't many **outlets** for the new product yet, and competition is **limited**.

3 — Growth

1) Sales grow fast. There are **new customers** and **repeat** customers.
2) **Economies of scale** mean the price of manufacturing a unit goes down the more you make, so **profits rise**.
3) The **pricing** strategy may change.
4) **Competitors** may be attracted to the market. Promotion points out **differences** from competitors.
5) The product is often **improved** or **developed**.
6) Rising sales encourage **more outlets** to stock the product.

4 — Maturity

1) **Sales** reach a **peak** and profitability increases because **fixed costs** of **development** have been **paid for**.
2) At **saturation**, sales may begin to drop depending on the product. Sales are more likely to drop for long-lasting products that customers do not need to replace regularly. The price is often reduced to stimulate **demand**, which reduces profits.
3) At this stage, there aren't many new customers. Some products are forced out of the market.

5 — Decline

1) The product doesn't **appeal** to customers any more. **Sales fall** rapidly and profits decrease.
2) On the other hand, the product may just stay profitable if **promotional costs** are **low** enough.
3) If sales carry on falling, the product is **withdrawn** or **sold** to another business. This is called **divestment**.

Product Life Cycle

Cash Flow Depends on the Product Life Cycle stage

Cash flow is the difference between **money coming in** and **money going out**. Money comes in from **investment** (especially at the start of the life cycle) and from **sales** (mostly later on). Money goes out as **fixed** and **variable costs**. If more money comes in than goes out, cash flow is **positive**. If more goes out than comes in, cash flow is **negative**.

1) At the **development** stage, cash flow is likely to be negative. Money has been spent on research and development and there aren't any sales to cover costs.

2) At **introduction**, cash flow is still negative. The product is likely to have **cost more** than it makes in sales. A **penetration pricing** strategy (see p.21) keeps cash flow down, but a **skimming** strategy improves cash flow.

3) As the product goes into the **growth** phase, **cash flow perks up**. Promotion costs should go down, and at the same times sales should be increasing.

4) When the product is in the **maturity** phase, cash flow is **positive**. Sales are **high** and unit **costs** are **low**.

5) In the **decline** phase, sales fall and this might lead to cash flow becoming **negative** again.

The Product Life Cycle stage affects Capacity Utilisation

1) **Capacity** is the **maximum amount** of a product that a business can produce at a particular point in time.

2) **Capacity utilisation** is **how much** of the capacity a business is using.

3) Before a business launches a product, it has to work out how many it'll need to make to fulfil **demand** at the **peak** of the life cycle. It should have those **production resources** in place at the **beginning** of the product life cycle — it's less upheaval than installing new production line machinery every few weeks to keep up with demand.

4) **Capacity utilisation** at **introduction** is **low**. *See p.70-71 for more on capacity utilisation.*

Extension Strategies keep a product Going Strong for Longer

Extension strategies try to prolong the life of the product by changing the **marketing mix**. They include:

1) **Product development** — businesses **improve**, reformulate or **redesign** a product. They can change the design of **packaging** to make it look more up-to-date. They can make **special editions** of the product.

2) **Market development** — businesses can find **new markets** or **new uses** for existing products, for example by aiming a product at a new market **segment** (e.g. selling baby oil and baby powder to adults).

3) A business can change the way the product's **distributed** — by selling through the **Internet**, selling through **supermarkets** or convenience stores, etc.

4) A business can change the way the product's **priced**.

5) A business can change the way they **promote** the product — by running a new **ad campaign**, for example.

> **Decline isn't inevitable** — it's usually caused by products becoming obsolete, changing consumer tastes or poor marketing. Quality products with excellent original design (e.g. Coca Cola) can carry on selling for **years**.

Practice Questions

Q1 What are the stages of the product life cycle?
Q2 What happens to cash flow during the growth stage of a product's life cycle?
Q3 What are extension strategies?
Q4 At what stage of a typical product life cycle does the product pay for its development costs?

Exam Questions

Q1 Describe what happens to cash flow during a product's life cycle. (5 marks)

Q2 To what extent are declining sales inevitable for products? (10 marks)

No product can live for ever — except maybe the KitKat... or the wheel...

There's a lot to learn on these pages, I'll give you that. If you take it step by step, it's fairly straightforward — it just goes through the product life cycle and says what's going on at each stage. If you know the product life cycle inside out, it won't be so hard to learn the bits about cash flow and capacity utilisation.

New Product Development

There's a lot to think about before bringing a new product onto the market. Businesses need the right mix of new, growing and mature products. **These two pages are for AQA, OCR and Edexcel.**

New Products can be great for a business

New products are usually completely new and distinct. But they can also be an **adaptation** of an existing product, an **imitation** of a competitor's product or a "**simulated adaptation**" (something which **looks** new, but isn't really new). They can be good for business for a number of reasons:

1) New products can bring in **new customers**.

2) They give a **competitive** advantage.

3) New products often fill a **gap in the market** — something that consumers **would like**, but that doesn't exist yet.

"It's a pair of glasses with a beverage holder attachment. It's new."

New Product Development includes Several Stages

1) **Ideas stage** — Market researchers look for a **gap in the market**, and figure out how a new product can best meet customer needs. The business does **research and development** (R&D) and analyses **competitor** products.

2) **Screening stage** — The business analyses the idea for the new product to see if it's **easy to market**, and to see if it'll make a **profit**. Market researchers find out what **consumers think** about the potential new product. A **prototype** is made to find out what the new product will really look like in real life.

The relative importance of formal and functional design depends on the product and the market.

3) **Product development stage** — The prototype is turned into a saleable product. The **functional design** of the product (its **structure** and how it **works**) and the **formal design** (its **appearance**) are tuned up and made as good as possible.

4) **Value analysis** — The business tries to make the product good **value** for money. They look at the economy of **making**, **warehousing** and **distributing** the product to make sure the whole process will be **efficient** and value for money — for the **business** and for the **consumer**.

5) **Testing** — Just before launch, the product is tested. A small batch of **pilot products** are made. Market research investigates **customer reactions** to the pilot products. If the public like it, the **production line** is tooled up to make the product. All systems are go — the business **launches** the product.

New product development is **expensive**. **Limited money** often puts the brakes on development. Sometimes it turns out that the product is **too expensive** to make and wouldn't be profitable.

Most new products Fail — it's better to fail Sooner rather than Later

1) If it looks like a product's going to fail, it's **abandoned**. It's better to put a failing product out of its misery instead of letting it drag on, **waste money** and ruin staff **morale**.

2) Some products reach the market but **still fail**. This can be because of **poor market research**, **defects** in the product, **competitors** having a better product, problems with **distribution**, higher than expected **costs**, **changes** to the **market** or plain old **lousy marketing**.

Product Portfolio Analysis

Businesses need a *Variety* of *Products* — a *Mixed Product Portfolio*

1) A **product line** consists of related products with similar characteristics, uses or target customers.

2) The **product mix** is the **combination** of all the **product lines** that a business produces.

3) Businesses aim to have a **mixed product portfolio** with a variety of different products, all at different stages of the product life cycle. That way if one product fails, the business should still be able to depend on the others.

The *Boston Matrix* is a model of *Portfolio Analysis*

Each circle in the matrix represents one product. The size of each circle represents the sales revenue of the product.

The Boston Matrix compares **market growth** with **market share**.

1) All **new products** are **question marks** (sometimes called **problem children** or **wildcats**) and they have small market share and high growth. These aren't profitable yet and could succeed or fail. They need **heavy marketing** to give them a chance. A business can do various things with question marks — **brand building**, **harvesting** (maximising sales or profit in the short term) or **divestment** (selling off the product).

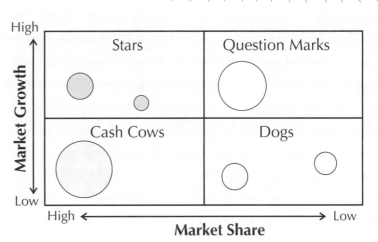

2) **Stars** have high market growth and high market share. They're in their profitable **growth** phase and have the most potential. They're future cash cows.

3) **Cash cows** have high market share but low market growth. They're in their **maturity** phase. They've already been promoted and they're produced in high volumes, so costs are low. Cash cows bring in plenty of **money**.

4) **Dogs** have low market share and low market growth. They're pretty much a lost cause. The business will either harvest profit in the short term, or sell them off.

The *Boston Matrix* is a useful tool

The Boston Matrix lets a business see if it has a good balanced **product portfolio**. A balanced product portfolio means that a business can use money from its **cash cows** to **invest** in its **question marks** so they can become **stars**.

The Boston Matrix **isn't infallible**. A product's **cash flow** and **profit** may be **different** from what the matrix suggests (e.g. a dog may have strong cash flow and be profitable despite falling sales).

Practice Questions

Q1 What are the stages of new product development?

Q2 Give examples of three things that a business should find out before marketing a new product.

Q3 Why are cash cows preferred to dogs?

Q4 What can a business do to its question marks to turn them into stars?

Exam Questions

Q1 Describe how a business seeks to minimise risk before launching a new product. (5 marks)

Q2 Discuss the usefulness of the Boston Matrix to a biscuit manufacturer. (10 marks)

The Boston Matrix — unlike the third Matrix film, you can understand it...

There's a lot for businesses to plan before they launch a new product — they have to be as sure as they can be that the product won't be a flop. The terminology of the Boston Matrix is a bit "different" but was designed to make some kind of sense — you milk cash cows for money, question marks are products you aren't sure of yet, dogs are... dogs.

Elasticity of Demand

Elasticity of demand means the way that demand for a product changes. It's a bit economics-ey, but not to worry ...
These pages are for all of you — AQA, OCR and Edexcel.

Demand depends on Several Factors

1) The **price of the product** affects demand. As the price goes up, the demand tends to go down. As the price goes down, demand goes up.

2) The **price of similar products** affects demand. When one manufacturer increases its prices, demand for **cheaper competitor products** tends to **rise**.

3) **Customer income** affects demand. When people have **more money to spend**, there's more demand.

4) **Seasonality** affects demand. The demand for soft drinks is greater in the **summer**.

5) Successful **marketing** stimulates demand.

Price Elasticity of Demand shows how Demand changes with Price

1) **Price elastic** products have a **large % change in demand** for a **small % change in price**.

2) **Price <u>in</u>elastic** products are the opposite — there's a **small % change in demand** for a **big % change in price**.

$$\text{Price elasticity of demand} = \frac{\text{\% change in quantity demanded}}{\text{\% change in price}}$$

Basically, as price goes up demand falls, and vice versa.

Example: A price **rise** of **10%** results in a **30% reduction** in demand.

$$\text{Price elasticity of demand} = \frac{-30\%}{+10\%} = -3$$

Price **elastic**, because the price elasticity of demand is **more than 1** (ignoring the minus sign).

Example: A price **reduction** of **20%** results in a **5% increase** in demand.

$$\text{Price elasticity of demand} = \frac{+5\%}{-20\%} = -0.25$$

Price **inelastic**, because the price elasticity of demand is **less than 1**.

3) Price elasticity of demand is **always negative**. This is because a positive change in price causes a negative change in demand, and a negative change in price causes a positive change in demand. There's always a minus sign in there somewhere...

4) If price elasticity of demand is **greater than 1** (ignoring the minus sign), the product is **price elastic**. If price elasticity of demand is **less than 1**, it's **price inelastic**. So, -5 means price elastic and -0.25 means price inelastic.

It can be Hard to Work Out price elasticity of demand

1) Estimating price elasticity of demand is **difficult** because price isn't the **only** factor affecting demand. An increase in demand for ice cream could be partly down to **hot weather** and a good **advertising** campaign.

2) Businesses use **primary market research** (see p.12) to ask people if they'd buy a product for a **higher** or **lower price**. This gives an idea of the relationship between **price** and **demand**. **However**, surveys can be **unreliable** (people generally say they'd like things a bit cheaper).

3) The values used in price elasticity calculations may be wrong. The calculations are often based on **estimates** of % change in price and demand, or on **unrepresentative** data. The market may have **changed** since data was collected

Price elasticity of demand Depends on Ease of Switching Brands

1) If a consumer can **easily switch** to a **competitor** product, the demand will be **price elastic**. A **rise in price** will result in customers jumping ship and buying the **competitor's product** instead.

2) Businesses try to **differentiate** their products to create **brand loyalty**. **Loyal** customers won't switch even if the price goes up, so this makes the demand **less** price elastic.

3) It's easier for customers to switch if they can **compare prices** and find cheaper alternatives. The **Internet** makes it easier to switch and **increases price elasticity**.

4) People tend not to switch to alternatives in the **short term**. They **take time** to get **fed up** with a product.

5) **Product types** tend to be **price inelastic**, but individual **brands** tend to be **price elastic**. For example, **petrol** sales are **inelastic** because all cars need fuel. The sales of an **individual company's petrol** are **elastic** because motorists can easily go to a **cheaper filling station**.

Elasticity of Demand

Price Elasticity affects Revenue and Profit

1) **Sales revenue = price** of product × **quantity sold**. Price elasticity shows how price affects sales revenue.

2) If demand is **price elastic**, an **increase** in **price** will make **sales revenue go down**.
The **% decrease in sales** will be **more** than the **% increase in price**.

3) If price is **inelastic**, a rise in **price** will make **sales revenue go up**.
The % decrease in sales isn't big enough to offset the % increase in price.

4) If demand is **price elastic**, a business can **increase revenue** by reducing price, which then increases the number of sales. **But profit = revenue – cost**, and more sales often mean **higher costs**. The **profits** will only increase if the **rise in revenue** is **more** than the **rise** in **costs**.

5) If demand is **price inelastic**, increasing the price will make **sales go down slightly**, but **sales revenue go up**. Because there are **fewer sales**, there are **lower costs**. This means that there's **more profit**.

Income Elasticity of Demand shows how Demand changes with Income

When people earn **more money**, there's **more demand** for some products.
Funnily enough, there's **less demand** for other products.

$$\text{Income elasticity of demand} = \frac{\% \text{ change in quantity demanded}}{\% \text{ change in real incomes}}$$

Change in <u>real income</u> means change in income, taking into account how prices have changed (usually increased) over the same period (this is <u>inflation</u> — see p.96).

Example: A **rise** in income of **10%** results in a **5% increase** in demand.

$$\text{Income elasticity of demand} = \frac{+5\%}{+10\%} = +0.5$$

1) **Normal goods** have a **positive income elasticity of demand** that's **less than 1**. This means that as **income rises**, the **demand** for normal goods **rises** — but at a **slower rate** than the increase in income.

2) **Luxury goods** have a **positive income** elasticity of demand which is **more than 1**.
This means that the **demand for luxury goods** grows **faster** than the increase in income.

3) **Inferior goods** are things that people are more likely to buy when they're poor. For example, you're less likely to take a **bus** if you can afford your own **car**. If you can't afford **Heinz baked beans**, you might switch to a **cheaper supermarket value brand**. Inferior goods have a **negative income elasticity of demand** — which means **demand falls** when **income rises** and **demand rises** when **income falls**.

AQA ——————— *AQA*

AQA (side) *AQA* (side)

Elasticity helps a business make Choices

1) **Price elasticity** helps a manufacturer **decide** whether to **raise** or **lower** the price of a product.
They can see what might happen to the sales, and whether they'll need more or less staff.

2) **Income elasticity** helps a manufacturer see what'll happen to sales if the **economy** grows or shrinks.

Practice Questions

Q1 How is price elasticity of demand calculated?

Q2 Explain what the term "inferior goods" means.

Q3 What factors affect price elasticity of demand?

Answer on p.102.

Exam Questions

Q1 If a price rise of 5% results in a 10% reduction in demand what is the price elasticity of demand?
Is the product price elastic, or price inelastic? (3 marks)

Q2 Explain why the demand for luxury goods increases rapidly in times of economic boom. (4 marks)

<u>Rubber prices are usually the most elastic...</u>

All this "elasticity of demand" sounds complicated. All it is, really, is a way to put an actual number on how much price affects demand for a product, and how much income affects demand for a product. Take a bit of time to get your head around the sums. Try this one: a price rise of 2% results in a 5% reduction in demand. What's the price elasticity?

Budgets

Businesses make financial plans. They set targets for how much money they're going to make, and how much they're going to spend. Then they check to see how they've done. **These pages are for all boards: Edexcel, AQA and OCR.**

A *Budget* is a *Financial Plan* for the future

1) A **budget** forecasts **future earnings** and **future spending**, usually over a twelve month period.

2) Budgets allow managers to **control their spending**.

3) **Budget holders** are people **responsible** for generating or spending the money for each budget. For example, the budget holder of the marketing budget would be the head of the marketing department.

4) Department budgets are broken down into budgets for **specific activities**.

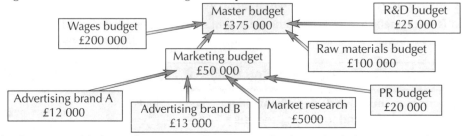

5) All functional budgets are added together to provide a **master budget** which forecasts total expenditure. The **master budget** helps businesses understand their **cash flow** situation, and the **detailed activity budgets** help local managers **control** and **coordinate** their work.

6) Budgets **set targets** that can be used to **control** or **motivate** staff, depending on management style. **Budgeting** is an important part of **management accounting** — see p.46.

The *Budget Setting* process involves *Research* and *Negotiation*

1) To set the **sales budget**, businesses **research** and **predict** how sales are going to go up and down through the year, so that they can make a good prediction of **sales revenue**.

2) To set the **production budget**, businesses research how labour costs, raw materials costs, taxes and inflation are going to go up over the year. They can then figure out the **costs** of producing the volume of product that they think they're going to sell.

3) Annual budgets are usually agreed by **negotiation** — when budget holders have a say in setting their budgets, they're **motivated** to achieve them.

4) Budgets should **stretch** the abilities of the business, but they must be **achievable**. **Unrealistically** high sales budgets or low production budgets will **demotivate** staff. No-one likes being asked to do the **impossible**.

Businesses *Monitor* their budgets

1) Once they've agreed the budget, budget holders **keep checking** performance against the budget. If there are any differences between the actual figures and the figures in the budget, managers need to sort them out.

2) The difference between the real figures and the ones in the budget is called the **variance**. Monitoring a budget by checking actual results against the budget is called **variance analysis**. There's more about this on p.34-35.

Budgets have *Advantages* and *Disadvantages*

Benefits of budgeting

- Budgets help **control** income and expenditure. They show where the money goes.
- Budgeting forces managers to frequently **review** their activities.
- Budgets let heads of department **delegate** authority to budget holders. Getting authority is **motivating**.
- Budgets allow different departments to **coordinate** their spending.
- Budgets help managers either **control** or **motivate** staff. Meeting a budget is **satisfying**.

Drawbacks of budgeting

- Budgeting can cause **resentment** and rivalry if departments have to compete with each other for money.
- Budgets can be **restrictive**. Fixed budgets can stop firms responding to changing market conditions.
- Budgeting is **time consuming**. Managers can get too preoccupied with setting and reviewing budgets, and forget to focus on the real issues of **winning business** and **understanding** the **customer**.

Budgets

Budgets can be **Updated Every Year** or developed from **Scratch**

Historical budgets are updated each year

1) This year's budget is based on a percentage increase or decrease from last year's budget. For example, a business expecting 10% revenue growth might add 10% to the advertising, wages and raw materials purchasing budgets.

2) Historical budgeting is **quick** and **simple** but it assumes that business conditions stay **unchanged** each year. This isn't always the case — for instance, a product at the introduction stage of its **life-cycle** needs more money spent on advertising than one in the growth or maturity stages.

AQA

Zero budgeting means starting from scratch each year

1) Budget holders **start** with a budget of £0, and have to **bid** (or beg) for money to spend on activities.

2) They have to **plan** all the year's activities, ask for money to spend on them, and be prepared to **justify** their requests to the finance director. Budget holders need good negotiating skills for this.

3) Zero budgeting takes much **longer** to complete than historical budgets.

4) If zero budgeting is done properly it's **more accurate** than historical budgeting.

AQA *AQA* *AQA* *AQA*

Fixed Budgets can make businesses **Inflexible**

1) **Fixed budgets** provide **discipline** and **certainty**. This is especially important for a business with **liquidity** problems — fixed budgets help control **cash flow**.

2) **Fixed budget** systems mean budget holders are expected to stick to their budget plans throughout the year — even though market conditions may change. Fixed budgets can **prevent** a firm reacting to **new opportunities** or **threats** that they didn't know about when they set the budget.

3) **Flexible budgeting** allows for budgets to be increased or reduced in response to significant changes in the market or the economy (i.e. not just on a whim, or because that £12 000 photocopier looked sooooo cool).

4) **Zero budgeting** gives a business more **flexibility** than **historical budgeting**.

Mary Lou had no problems with flexibility

Practice Questions

Q1 Give three examples of budgets that a business might set, stating what each would measure.

Q2 State three benefits and three drawbacks of using budgets.

Q3 What is historical budgeting?

Q4 Explain the difference between fixed and flexible budgets.

Exam Questions

Q1 To what extent might fixed budgets help a manufacturer in the fast-changing computer software sector? (15 marks)

Q2 (a) Discuss the benefits that setting a budget will have for a new business. (6 marks)
(b) Discuss the problems that a new business might have in setting budgets for the first time. (9 marks)

I set myself a word budget today and I'm just about to run out...

Budgets are the only way to keep an eye on what you're spending. This goes for ordinary folk like you and me as well as for businesses. Luckily, you aren't going to get marked on how good you are at budgeting — just on how well you understand what businesses have to do when they set a budget. Setting a budget involves lots of research and meetings, apparently.

Variances

Variance is the difference between actual and budgeted spend. Managers look at variances to help them understand and control business performance. ***These pages are for AQA.***

Variance is the *Difference* between *Actual* figures and *Budget* figures

1) A variance means the business is performing either **worse** or **better** than expected.

2) A **favourable variance** leads to **profits increasing**. If revenue's more than the budget says it's going to be, that's a favourable variance. If costs are below the cost predictions in the budget, that's a favourable variance.

3) An **adverse variance** is a difference that **reduces profits**. Selling fewer items than the sales budget predicts is an adverse variance. Spending more on an advert than the marketing budget allows is an adverse variance.

4) Variances **add up**. For example, if actual sales exceed budgeted sales by £3000 and expenditure on raw materials is £2000 below budget, there's a combined **favourable variance** of £5000. Or if £10 000 were spent on raw materials in a month when the budget was only £6000, that would create a £4000 **adverse variance**.

	Jan Budget	Jan Actual	Jan Variance	Feb Budget	Feb Actual	Feb Variance	Cumulative Variance
Revenue	£100k	£90k	£10k (A)	£110k	£110k	£0	£10k (A)
Wages	£40k	£30k	£10k (F)	£40k	£41k	£1k (A)	£9k (F)
Rent	£10k	£10k	£0	£10k	£11k	£1k (A)	£1k (A)
Other costs	£5k	£6k	£1k (A)	£5k	£6k	£1k (A)	£2k (A)
Total costs	£55k	£46k	£9k (F)	£55k	£58k	£3k (A)	£6k (F)

Variances can be calculated for each budget each month, for each budget as a running total, and for groups of budgets as a monthly or running total variance.

(A) means an adverse variance.
(F) means a favourable variance.

Variances can be *Bad* — even when they say you're doing *Better* than *Expected*

1) It's extremely important to spot adverse variances as **soon** as possible. It's important to find out which budget holder is responsible — and to take action to fix the problem.

2) It's **also** important to **investigate favourable variances**. Favourable variances may mean that the budget targets weren't **stretching** enough — so the business needs to set more **difficult targets**. The business also needs to understand **why** the performance is better than expected — if the department is **doing something right**, the business can **spread** this throughout the organisation.

Variances are caused by several factors — *Internal* and *External*

External Factors Cause Variance

1) **Competitor behaviour** and changing **fashions** may increase or reduce **demand** for products.

2) Changes in the **economy** can change how much workers wages cost the business.

3) The cost of **raw materials** can go up — e.g. if a harvest fails.

Internal Factors Cause Variance

1) Improving **efficiency** causes **favourable** variances, e.g. introducing automated production equipment or bulk-buying raw materials.

2) However, a business might **overestimate** the amount of money it can save by streamlining its production methods.

3) A business might **underestimate** the **cost** of making a change to its organisation, for example it might not take account of the cost of **training** employees to use a new computer system.

4) Changing the selling price changes sales revenue. If a business cuts the price of its products after it's **already** set the budget, there'll be a **variance**.

5) Internal causes of variance are a **serious concern**. They suggest that the **communication** in a business needs improvement.

Variances

Variance Analysis means Identifying and Explaining variances

1) Variance analysis means **spotting** variances and figuring out **why** they've happened, so that action can be taken to fix them.

2) **Small** variances aren't a big problem. They can actually help to **motivate** employees. Staff try to **catch up** and sort out small **adverse** variances themselves. Small **favourable** variances can motivate staff to **keep on** doing whatever they were doing to create a favourable variance.

3) **Large** variances can **demotivate**. Staff don't work hard if there are large favourable variances — they **don't see the need**. Staff can get demotivated by a large **adverse** variance — they may feel that the task is **impossible**, or that they've **already failed**.

Businesses have to Do Something about variances

1) Businesses can either change what the **business** is doing to make it fit the budget, or change the **budget** to make it fit what the **business** is doing.

2) **Flexible** budgets **can** be changed. **Fixed** budgets **can't be changed**.

3) Businesses need to **beware** of chopping and changing the budget **too much**.

4) Changing the budget **removes certainty** — which removes one of the big benefits of budgets.

5) Altering budgets can also make them **less motivating** — when staff start to expect that management will change targets instead of doing something to change performance, they don't see the point in trying any more.

Businesses Act to Fix Adverse Variances

1) They can change the **marketing mix**. They can **cut prices** to increase sales — they'll only do this if the demand is price elastic (see p.30). They can **update** the product to make it more attractive to customers. They can look for a **new market** for the product. They can change the **promotional strategy** — e.g. by advertising the product more or doing point of sales promotion.

2) They can **streamline production** to make it more **efficient**, so costs are reduced.

3) They can try to motivate **employees** to **work harder**.

4) They can try to cut costs by asking their **suppliers** for a **better deal**.

Businesses Act to Fix Favourable Variances

1) If the variance is because of **increased productivity** in one part of the business, they try to get everyone else doing whatever was **responsible** for the improvement.

2) If the favourable variance is caused by a **pessimistic** budget, they make sure that they set more **ambitious targets** next time.

Practice Questions

Q1 Define variance.
Q2 State three examples of an adverse variance.
Q3 Explain what might cause a favourable variance on a raw materials purchasing budget.
Q4 How do businesses deal with variances?

Answer on p.102.

Exam Questions

Q1 Using the figures in the table on p.34, calculate monthly and cumulative variances for March. Assume all budgets remain the same as February, and that actual sales are £120k, wages are £39k, rent is £11k and total costs are £55k. (6 marks)

Q2 What does your answer to Q1 suggest about the budget planning process for this company? (6 marks)

Variance is one of those words that looks odd if you stare at it enough...

Variance variance variance variance variance... ahem... anyway. As well as knowing what businesses do when they set a budget, you need to know what they do when the real life results don't quite match up to the budget prescriptions. Do they panic like you or I probably would — no they do not. They sort things out and get them shipshape again.

Cost and Profit Centres

Businesses can look at sales budgets and production budgets for the whole of the business — or they can look at one part of the business in isolation and work out how much money it's spending, and how much money it's making.
These pages are just for AQA. *Everyone else — you can run along. See you on page 38.*

Businesses set budgets for **Parts** of the business — **Cost** and **Profit Centres**

> All cost and profit centres are is a **way to work out budgets** for a particular **part** of a business. With a **cost centre**, you can work out costs, so you can set a **cost budget**. With a **profit centre**, you can work out **costs** and **revenues**. This means you can set a budget for how much money you want that part of the business to **bring in** over a year, as well as how much money you want it to **cost** that year. It's that simple.

1) Parts of a business that directly **incur costs** can be treated as **cost centres**. The business can identify costs, measure them, and **monitor** them against a **mini-budget** that just applies to that part of the business.

2) Parts of a business that directly **generate revenue** as well as costing money can be treated as **profit centres**. The business can work out the **profit** or **loss** they're making by subtracting the **costs** from the **revenues**.

3) The IT department of a business is an example of a **cost centre**. Managers **can** work out the **costs** of IT technician wages and new computer upgrades. They **can't** work out the **revenue** that the IT department earns, because they **don't charge** other departments for providing IT support.

4) A chain of shops can treat **each shop** as a **profit centre**. The business owner **can** work out the **costs** of stock, rent and staff wages for each shop, and also work out **sales revenue** for each shop.

5) Manufacturers can treat each **product line** as a profit centre. Individual **brands** can also be profit centres.

Cost and profit centres have **Several Uses**

① **Financial decision making**

1) Overall company profits don't tell senior managers exactly **where** the profits are being made. Cost and profit centres let managers **compare** costs of different parts of the business. They can try to make the less cost-efficient parts **more efficient**.

2) Managers can use **cost centres** to help them **set prices** — once they know the cost, they can set the price so that they'll make a profit.

② **Organisation and control**

1) Managers can use cost and profit centre information when they want to change the **organisation** of the business. They can focus on the **profitable** areas.

2) Managers can set **cost limits** and **profit targets** to coordinate staff and **focus** their minds on specific activities. They can link **pay** and **bonuses** to meeting profit targets and keeping costs down in each department, team or shop.

③ **Motivation**

1) Cost and profit centres with their own budgets allow **junior managers** and **employees** to control budgets.

2) Profit share schemes mean employees and managers within profit centres can earn **bonus** payments when profits are good — but this can backfire if profits aren't as good as expected.

> Senior managers <u>delegate</u> budget setting to junior managers — they allow them the authority to make budget decisions. P.63 has more on delegation.

Example: When British Airways came under intense pressure from budget airlines, the company realised they had to **cut costs** to compete. They calculated costs, revenues, profit and loss for each **route**. Managers **closed** the **loss-making** routes and put money toward **increasing** the services on the more **profitable** routes. The marketing department were set targets intended to motivate them and generate more customers for these routes. Company performance started to improve.

Cost and Profit Centres

Businesses Define cost and profit centres in Different Ways

Cost and profit centres can be defined by:

1) **Product**, e.g. a high street **clothing** company might monitor costs and revenues for each product, so it could know how much profit or loss different lines of clothing contributed to the business.

2) **Factory**, e.g. **car companies** use factories as a cost and profit centre so they know what percentage of costs and profits each factory represents to the business. This information is useful if the business needs to **downsize** — they can close the **least profitable** factories and keep the profitable ones going.

3) **Location**, e.g. **supermarkets** that know how much revenue and profit each **store** generates are better informed when it comes to targeting geographic areas for future expansion. They can choose areas with **profitable** stores for expansion.

4) **Person**, e.g. companies with a sales force will usually monitor **each salesperson** as a profit centre. Salespeople are very **expensive** to employ — so a business will be keen to make sure none of them are **costing** the business **more** money than they generate in profit.

Cost Centres Must Include Indirect Costs

Indirect costs are **overheads** — things like senior managers' salaries, rent for a factory or shop, etc. They're all the costs that a business has to pay out which aren't directly tied to a specific product. There's more about direct and indirect costs on p.42.

Cost and profit centres have Advantages and Disadvantages

Advantages of cost and profit centres	Disadvantages of cost and profit centres
Managers can **easily spot** the successful and unsuccessful parts of the business.	Giving junior employees responsibility for setting budgets can be **too much** for them to handle. They'll need financial **training** first.
Local managers can take decisions to **suit** their cost or profit centre. They can set prices for the **local market**.	It can be **hard** to divide a business into cost and profit centres. Sharing out the costs of **overheads** like rent is particularly tricky.
Meeting targets on a **local** level can be **more motivating** than working towards a **distant** national target.	There's **rivalry** between cost and profit centres in a business. If it goes too far, it can be a problem — branches could be more concerned with beating each other's profits than with customers.

Cost and profit centres don't suit all businesses. Owners or leaders who like to **make all the decisions** won't be happy about **delegating** budget setting. Businesses without **able junior staff** won't be able to **handle** cost and profit centres. Also, it often isn't worth working out cost and profit centres for a business which just sells **one kind of product**.

Practice Questions

Q1   What is a cost centre?

Q2   Would the maintenance and facilities management department be a cost centre or a profit centre?

Q3   Give two reasons why a business might use cost and profit centres.

Q4   State three ways in which a business can divide its operations up into profit centres.

Q5   Give two drawbacks of using cost and profit centres.

Exam Questions

Q1   Why might a small business owner decide not to establish cost and profit centres for their business?   (6 marks)

Q2   Tanya Richards owns and manages four beauty salons, and runs each salon as a profit centre. She also has a small office where she and her assistant look after all the admin, accounting and marketing for the business.
(a) Why does Tanya run her office as a cost centre, not as a profit centre?   (2 marks)
(b) To what extent do you think running the salons as profit centres will motivate Tanya's staff? Explain your answer.   (11 marks)

Need profits? Go to the local profit centre — if only it were that simple...

Cost and profit centres are especially good for businesses like banks, supermarkets and manufacturers — it makes a lot of sense to divide these businesses up into individual bank branches, individual stores and individual product lines. Don't go thinking that profit centres and cost centres are opposites — it's just that you can't measure profit for a cost centre.

Cash Flow

Cash flow is money flowing in and out of a business. It's vital to have enough money to meet your immediate debts — otherwise the people you owe money to start getting very cross. **These pages are for AQA, OCR and Edexcel.**

Cash Flow isn't the same as Profit

1) **Cash flow** is all money flowing **into** and **out of** the business over a period of time, calculated at the **exact time** the cash physically **enters** or **leaves** the bank account or till.

2) **Profit** is calculated by recording all transactions that will **lead** to cash going **in** or **out** of the business at some point in the **future**. Selling something on credit counts as profit now, but it won't count as cash flow until the customer actually pays for it.

The Cash Flow Cycle is the Gap between Money Going Out and Coming In

1) Businesses need to **pay money out** for fixed assets (e.g. buildings, machinery and vehicles) and operating costs to fulfil an order **before** they **get paid** for that order. New businesses **need money** to spend on start-up costs **before** they've even started to get any sales at all.

2) This **delay** between money going out and money coming in is the **cash flow cycle** — as in the diagram.

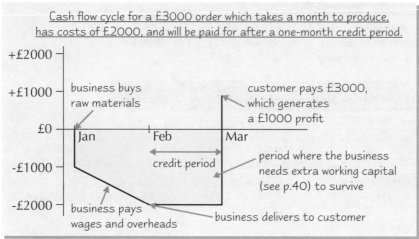

Cash flow cycle for a £3000 order which takes a month to produce, has costs of £2000, and will be paid for after a one-month credit period.

> Bankruptcy is for sole traders/partnerships, and insolvency is for companies.

3) It's important to make sure there's always **enough money** available to pay **suppliers** and **wages**. Not paying suppliers and employees can be something of a **disaster**.

4) If a business **produces too much**, they'll have to **pay** suppliers and staff **so much** that they'll go **bankrupt** or **insolvent** before they have the chance to **get paid** by their customers. This is called **overtrading**.

Cash flow calculations are pretty much **the most important thing** to a business in the **short term**. Businesses need cash to survive. Looking at the long term, profit is important — making profit is the main objective for businesses.

Businesses have Various Canny Tricks to Improve cash flow

The first three measures below aim to give businesses **improved working capital control** (see p.40).

1) Businesses try to **reduce the time** between **paying** suppliers and **getting money** from customers. They try to get their **suppliers** to give them a **longer** credit period — and give their **customers** a **shorter** credit period. It's important to **balance** the need to manage cash flow with the need to keep suppliers and customers **happy** — you don't want customers to go elsewhere.

2) Businesses can try to hold less **stock**, so less cash is tied up in stock (see p.76-77 for more on stock).

3) **Credit controllers** keep **debtors** in control. They set credit limits and remind debtors to pay up.

4) **Debt factoring** gives instant cash to businesses whose customers haven't paid their invoices. Banks and other financial institutions act as **debt factoring agents**. The agent pays the business about **80%** of the value of the invoice as an **instant cash advance**. The agent gets the customer to pay up, and then **keeps** about **5%** of the value of the invoice — debt factoring costs money.

5) **Sale and leaseback** is when businesses **sell** equipment to **raise capital**, and then **lease** (rent) the equipment back. That way, they get a big **lump sum** from the sale, and pay a **little** bit of money each month for the lease of the equipment. Of course, they don't get to own the equipment again unless they get enough cash to buy it back — and they have to pay the lease in the meantime.

AQA — AQA — AQA — AQA

Cash Flow

Businesses make Cash Flow Forecasts to help them make decisions

1) **Cash flow forecasts** (also called cash budgets) show the amount of money that managers **expect** to **come into** the business and **flow out** of the business over a period of time in the **future**.

2) Managers can use cash flow forecasts to **make sure** they always have **enough** cash around to pay **suppliers** and **employees**. Managers who forecast cash flow can **predict** when they'll be **short of cash**, and arrange a **loan** or **overdraft** in time to cover the difficult spot.

3) Businesses show cash flow forecasts to **banks** and venture capitalists when trying to get **loans** and other finance. Cash flow forecasts prove that the business has an idea of where it's going to be in the future.

Here's how to Construct and Interpret a Cash Flow Forecast

Example: A new business starts up with a loan of £18 000 and £5000 of capital. It expects to sell £5000 worth of products in January, £35 000 in February, £35 000 in March and £40 000 in April. All customers will be granted a **one month credit period**. Wages and rent will cost £15 000 each month, and other costs are expected to be £5000 in January, £8000 in February, £2000 in March and £2000 in April.

This shows cash coming in from sales and from the initial start-up loan.

This shows cash going out to pay for the firm's costs.

Net cash flow = total revenue – total costs

	Item	Jan	Feb	Mar	Apr
Cash in	Sales revenue		£5000	£35 000	£35 000
	Other cash in	£18 000			
	Total cash in	**£18 000**	**£5000**	**£35 000**	**£35 000**
Cash out	Wages and rent	£15 000	£15 000	£15 000	£15 000
	Advertising/other costs	£5000	£8000	£2000	£2000
	Total costs	**£20 000**	**£23 000**	**£17 000**	**£17 000**
Net monthly cash flow	Net cash flow	(£2000)	(£18 000)	£18 000	£18 000
	Opening balance	£5000	£3000	(£15 000)	£3000
	Closing balance	**£3000**	**(£15 000)**	**£3000**	**£21 000**

April's sales aren't included because they won't be paid for until May, by the way.

Figures in brackets are negative.

According to this, the business will have £21 000 in the bank by the end of April. But it'll still owe £18 000 from the start-up loan ...

The opening balance is money in the bank at the start, in this case £5000.

Closing balance = opening balance + net cash flow

The closing balance for last month is this month's opening balance.

... and this is only a forecast. How would February sales of, say, £25 000 affect the outcome?

For **OCR** and **AQA**, you have to be able to draw up a cash flow forecast — although it's likely to be limited to filling in a couple of missing figures. For **Edexcel**, you just have to interpret one that's already drawn up for you.

Cash Flow Forecasting isn't always accurate

1) Cash flow forecasts can be based on **false assumptions** about what's going to happen.

2) Circumstances can **change suddenly** after the forecast's been made. **Costs** can **go up**. Machinery can **break down** and need mending. **Competitors** can put their prices up or down, which **affects sales**.

3) Good cash flow forecasting needs lots of **experience** and lots of **research** into the market.

4) A **false forecast** can have **disastrous** results. A business that runs out of cash can go **bankrupt** or **insolvent**.

Practice Questions

Q1 What's the difference between profit and cash flow?

Q2 Give two reasons why a cash flow forecast is useful to someone setting up their own small business.

Q3 How do you work out: a) the net cash flow, and b) the closing balance in a cash flow forecast?

Exam Questions

Q1 Analyse the ways in which a business can improve its cash flow. (9 marks)

Q2 To what extent can a business successfully and accurately predict future cash flow? Explain your answer. (12 marks)

Dunno 'bout you, but cash flows through my wallet like water...

Cash flow is vitally important for a business. Without it, businesses can go bankrupt or insolvent.
Make sure you understand how to calculate the figures in the forecast box on this page.
It can be slightly tricky to start with, so go slowly, and go over it a few times until you really get it.

Sources of Finance

There's a mighty big range of possible sources of finance out there. **These two pages are for AQA and Edexcel.**

Businesses need **Finance** for **Working Capital** and **Capital Expenditure**

1) **Capital expenditure** means money used to buy **fixed assets**. These are things used over and over again to produce goods or services for sale — e.g. **factories** and **equipment**. Businesses need capital expenditure to **start up**, to **expand** and to **replace** worn out equipment.

2) **Working capital** (or **revenue expenditure**) is the cash needed to pay for the daily running of a business. It's used to pay wages, suppliers, electricity/gas bills, business rates etc. The amount of working capital is predicted using the **cash flow forecast** (see p.39).

3) **Capital expenditure** allows a business to **grow**. **Working capital** allows a business to **survive**. All businesses need **both** types of finance.

> Expenditure is a fancy way of saying "spending".

Edexcel — Edexcel

1) **Working capital** is the **difference** between **current assets** and **current liabilities**.

2) **Current assets** are things a business **owns** that can be **turned into cash** very **soon** — things like **stock**, money that's **owed** to the business by debtors, and **cash itself**.

3) **Current liabilities** are things that the business will **soon** have to shell out cash to **pay for** — things like money it **owes** to creditors, an **overdraft**, money it has to pay to **shareholders** soon.

4) It's **very important** to have enough working capital. **Without** enough working capital, a firm can't pay the **bills** quickly, can't buy in **bulk** (so no bulk **discounts**), can't offer customers a long enough **credit** period, can't **develop** new products — and it gets a **bad reputation** and **annoys** its creditors.

Debtors = people who owe you money. Creditors = people who you owe money to.

Edexcel

Finance can be **Internal** or **External**, **Short-term** or **Long-term**, **Debt** or **Equity**

1) **Internal** finance is capital made available **within** the firm by cutting costs, or by putting **profits from trading** back into the business. Internal capital is always quite **limited**.

2) **External** finance is capital raised **outside** the business.

3) Ways of raising external capital include **selling shares**, asking the bank for an **overdraft** and getting a **loan** from a bank or a venture capitalist.

> Here, "long-term" describes when a <u>debt</u> is due to be repaid. But the money may be used to meet medium-term <u>needs</u> — see p41.

1) **Short-term finance** is capital that's raised, used, and paid back quickly. A mechanic using a **bank overdraft** to buy a new car engine then selling the car and repaying the overdraft within a few **weeks** is a good example. Businesses use short-term finance to give them **extra working capital** so that they can pay their bills while they're waiting for their customers to pay up.

2) **Long-term finance** is capital that's paid back over a period of **more than one year**.

1) **Debt** is money **borrowed** from someone. It has to be **paid back**, with **interest**. Debt allows new and small businesses to buy things that they couldn't afford otherwise — a business can grow faster if it doesn't have to save up to buy equipment and raw materials.

2) **Equity** capital is money received from **selling shares**. This raises large amounts of capital quickly and it doesn't need paying back. The drawback of raising money by selling shares is that the **shareholders control the business**. It's easier to control a business owned by a few shareholders than a business owned by lots of shareholders. Shareholders get a little **slice** of the **profits**, too.

3) The proportion of a business that's financed through debt rather than equity is called **gearing**. **Highly geared** firms financed mainly through **debt** can grow quickly — but they'll need to use a lot of their profits to pay back the debt and the **interest** on it. There's more about gearing on p.51.

There are **Three Main Ways** to raise **Internal Capital**

1) **Profit** can be retained and built up over the years for **later investment**.

2) Businesses can **sell** some of their **assets** to generate capital. This is called **rationalisation**.

3) A business can find some internal capital by **reducing working capital** (money needed for the basic running of the business). They do this by reducing the amount of **stock** they hold, **delaying** payments to **suppliers** and **speeding up** payments from **customers**. The saving can go towards future spending. The amount of capital a business can get from tightening its belt like this is **limited**.

Sources of Finance

External Finance can be for Short, Medium and Long Term Needs

External finance can increase working capital in the short term

1) **Trade credit** is where a business negotiates a **delay** between **receiving** raw materials or stock and **paying** for them. **30 days** is a typical credit period. Larger businesses may negotiate longer periods.

2) **Overdrafts** are where a bank lets a business have a negative amount of money in its account, up to an overdraft limit. They're easily arranged and **flexible** — the business can borrow any amount up to the limit. Overdrafts are usually only suitable for a **short** period, as banks charge a **lot** of **interest** on them.

3) **Debt factoring** is a service that banks and other financial institutions offer. They take **unpaid invoices** off the hands of the business, and give them instant **cash** payment (of around 80% of the value of the invoice). They collect payment from the individual or company who should have paid the invoice, and **keep** some of the money as a **fee**. See p.38 for more on debt factoring as a way of improving cash flow.

External finance is used for medium-term needs — usually between 1 and 5 years

1) **Loans** have lower interest charges than overdrafts — they're suitable for **medium-term** finance. Loans are repaid in monthly instalments. Banks need security for a loan, usually in the form of property. If the business doesn't repay the loan, the bank can sell the property from under them to get their money back.

2) **Leasing** is when a business **rents** fixed assets like cars and office equipment instead of **buying** them. Leasing means paying a smallish amount each month instead of shelling out a lot of money all in one go. Businesses can easily **upgrade** equipment or vehicles that they're leasing. In the **long run**, leasing works out **more expensive** than buying, though.

External finance can also be used for long-term projects

1) **Debentures** are special kinds of long-term **loan** with low **fixed interest rates** and **fixed repayment dates**.

2) **Grants** are money from local government and some business charities — they don't have to be repaid. To qualify for a grant, businesses usually have to be creating **new jobs**, setting up in **deprived** areas or being started by **young people**.

3) A limited company can sell **shares** in the business. Shareholders can get a share of the profits, called a **dividend**. The share price goes up if the business does well, so shareholders can sell their shares at a profit. **Ordinary shares** give a **variable** dividend each year that depends on how much profit the company has made. **Preference shares** give a **fixed** dividend each year. Ordinary shareholders stand to benefit more from a good performance, but preference shareholders get the first bite at the profits — if profits are low, ordinary shareholders don't get much dividend.

4) **Venture capitalists** provide capital by giving loans and by buying shares. Venture capital is particularly suitable for business start-ups or expansion.

AQA and Edexcel ———— *AQA and Edexcel*

A company's financial statements give details of where its money came from. You'll find sources of finance like debentures, shares, overdrafts and bank loans detailed on the balance sheet. See p.47.

(side margin: AQA and Edexcel — AQA and Edexcel — AQA and Edexcel)

Practice Questions

Q1 State two reasons why a business needs finance.

Q2 Explain what is meant by the term 'debt factoring'.

Q3 What types of businesses are most likely to qualify for grants?

Q4 What is the difference between an overdraft and a loan?

Exam Questions

Q1 Describe three types of finance that might be suitable for financing the launch of a cyber-café business. (6 marks)

Q2 Discuss why most businesses finance growth and expansion with a mixture of internal and external finance. (8 marks)

Unfortunately you can't sell shares in being slightly bored with BS...

I was planning on financing my business with £1 coins from the back of the sofa. Guess not, then. All kidding aside, it's worth knowing about the different kinds of finance that businesses have at their disposal. Remember, a lot of it depends on whether the business wants money for the short term or the long term, and if it's for fixed assets or working capital.

Costs

A business which didn't have a clue about how much its products cost to produce would be in a rather sorry state. They wouldn't know how much profit they were making for a start. **These pages are for Edexcel, AQA and OCR.**

Costs, *Revenue* and *Profit* are all *Related*

> Revenue = quantity sold × selling price per item
> Profit = revenue – costs

You need to have those two facts firmly jammed into your head.

1) Revenue is the value of sales — it's sometimes just called "**sales**". It's also called **turnover**.

2) Profit depends on the **profit margin**. The profit margin is the percentage of the selling price that's profit. If a teapot costs £6 to produce and sells for £8, the profit margin is **25%**. $\frac{8-6}{8} \times 100 = 25\%$

3) **Revenue** and **profit** are affected by both **sales volume** and **price**. The amount of sales you lose by putting the price up varies — see **price elasticity of demand** on p.30-31.

4) Businesses can do two things with profits. They can **give them to the shareholders** as dividend payments or they can **re-invest** their profits in new activities.

5) **Shareholders** often want a **short-term** reward for supporting the business. In the long term, it's often better for the business to hold on to the profit and **re-invest** it in future projects.

Costs can be *Fixed* or *Variable*

1) **Fixed costs** don't change with output. I rather fondly imagine that's **why** they're called "fixed" costs. **Rent** on a factory, business **rates**, **senior managers' salaries** and the cost of **new machinery** are fixed costs. When output increases, a business makes more use of the facilities it's already got. The **cost** of those facilities **doesn't change**.

2) **Variable costs** rise and fall as output changes. Hourly **wages**, **raw materials** and the **packaging costs** for each product are all variable costs.

3) **Semi-variable** costs have fixed and variable parts. **Telephone bills** are good examples of **semi-variable** costs. Businesses have to pay a **fixed** amount for their phone line plus a **variable** amount depending on how many phone calls they've made.

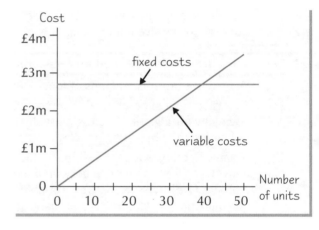

Large-scale Production *helps keep costs* Low

The more a business produces, the **lower** the **cost per unit** produced. The **fixed costs** are **shared out** between **more items**. The best way to show this is with an example:

There's more about this sort of thing on p.68. It's called "economies of scale".

> Superlec make microwave ovens. The fixed costs of running Superlec are £200 000.
> The variable costs of materials and labour are £15 per microwave.
>
> If Superlec make 5000 microwaves a year, the total production costs are... £200 000 + (£15 × 5000) = **£275 000**.
> The cost per microwave is £275 000 ÷ 5000 = **£55**.
>
> If Superlec make 20 000 microwaves a year, the total production costs are... £200 000 + (£15 × 20 000) = **£500 000**.
> The cost per microwave is £500 000 ÷ 20 000 = **£25**.

Costs can be *Direct* or *Indirect*

1) **Direct costs** are directly linked to a **product** or **service**. The cost of raw materials and the hourly wages paid to factory workers making a product are direct costs.

2) **Indirect costs** can't be directly linked to only one product or service. They're also called **overheads**. Wages and salaries paid to people who **aren't directly involved** in making the product (e.g. senior managers, canteen workers) are indirect costs, as are business rates and rent.

3) **Direct** costs are almost always **variable** costs. **Indirect** costs are almost always **fixed** costs.

4) **Gross profit** is what you get when you subtract **direct** costs from revenue.
Net profit is what you get when you subtract direct **and** indirect costs from revenue.

Costs

Businesses need to work out **Product Costs**

1) Businesses use **cost** information to set the **selling price** of their products and services (see p.21). They set the price to make sure they'll make **profits**. (Number of sales × price) – cost = profit.

2) If a business is a "**price taker**" in a very competitive market, it **doesn't have control** of the **selling price** of its products — it takes whatever price the market will pay. Businesses in this situation need accurate **costing** information to work out if it's **profitable** to make and sell a product at all.

3) Businesses set **budgets** (see p.32) which forecast how much costs are going to be over a year. Managers need to know what costs they're incurring **now**, so that they can know whether they're **meeting** the budget.

For each unit, **Costs = Direct Costs** + a share of the **Indirect Costs**

1) The **total costs** of making a product are the **direct costs** and the **indirect costs** added together. It can also be useful for a business to know the costs **per unit** of production — for example, it'll help when it comes to making decisions about whether to increase or decrease output.

2) There are several methods of working out the cost to a business of making a product, but the only one you need to know for AS level is **marginal costing** (and that's only for OCR anyway).

OCR — *OCR* — *OCR*

1) **Marginal costing** considers **direct costs** only — the change in costs when output is increased or decreased. **Overheads** are **ignored** in this calculation.

   Marginal costing is sometimes called <u>contribution costing</u>.

2) Instead, each sale is used to make a **contribution** to overheads. Once overheads are **covered**, all contribution is **profit** — see p.44.

3) The finance department works out the contribution each sale has to make, and how many sales are needed. Marginal costing is used to work out **break even** — see p.44 again.

4) Because marginal costing handles overheads **centrally**, it can lead to departments **not bothering** to **control** their own overheads.

OCR — *OCR*

Costs also relate to **Missed Opportunities**

Two cars... or 30 holidays... or 8000 McDonalds Value Meals...

1) **Opportunity cost** puts a value on a product or business decision in terms of what the business had to give up in order to have it. The opportunity cost of a **new ad campaign** might be a **refurbishment plan** for the office.

2) Businesses must **choose** where to spend their limited finance. Managers **compare opportunity costs** when making their decisions. The opportunity cost of an advert half way through an episode of Pop Idol might be five screenings of the same advert in the middle of Emmerdale.

Practice Questions

Q1 What is a profit margin?

Q2 Give three examples of a fixed cost.

Q3 What's a semi-variable cost? Give an example of one.

Q4 What's an opportunity cost?

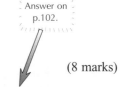
Answer on p.102.

Exam Questions

Q1 Analyse the reasons why a business might limit the amount of profit it pays out to shareholders. (8 marks)

Q2 Beth Brook Hats employs two hat makers, each at £280/week. Beth, as Managing Director, pays herself £400/week. The other fixed costs are £300/week. The variable costs of raw materials are £14 per hat. Hats sell for £50.
   (a) Draw a graph to show fixed, variable and total costs for outputs between 0 hats/week to 100 hats/week. (6 marks)
   (b) Calculate the profit that Beth is making at her current output level of 60 hats per week, assuming weekly sales match output. (4 marks)

If you don't learn this, it'll cost you...

Costs, revenue and profit are kind of at the heart of this section. They're pretty simple concepts, but they're used to work out everything else. You need to be able to classify costs as fixed or variable and direct or indirect. Remember that costs relate to things you gave up in order to buy something, not just the money you paid.

Break Even

Break even analysis is a great way of working out how much you need to sell to make profit. **For AQA, OCR and Edexcel.**

Breaking Even means Covering your Costs

1) **Break even point** is the level of sales a business needs to **cover their costs**. At this point, costs = revenue.

2) When sales are **below** the break even point, costs are more than revenue — the business makes a **loss**.
When sales are **above** the break even point, revenue exceeds costs — the business makes a **profit**.

3) **New businesses** should always do a **break even analysis** to **find** the break even point. Banks and venture capitalists **loaning** money to the business will need to **see** a break even analysis as part of the **business plan**.

4) **Established businesses** preparing to launch **new products** use break even analysis to work out how much **profit** they'll make, and also to predict the impact of the new activity on **cash flow** (see p.38-39).

Contribution is used to work out Break Even

1) **Contribution** is the difference between the **selling price** of a product and the **variable costs** it takes to produce it.

> Contribution per unit = selling price per unit – variable costs per unit

2) Contribution is used to **pay fixed costs**. The amount left over is profit.

3) **Break even** is the point where **contribution = fixed costs**.
Break even output is fixed costs over contribution per unit.

$$\text{Break even output} = \frac{\text{fixed costs}}{\text{contribution per unit}}$$

> **Example:** Harry sets up a business to print T-shirts. The **fixed costs** of premises and the T-shirt printers are **£3000**. The **variable costs** per T-shirt (the T-shirt, ink, wages) are **£5**. Each printed T-shirt sells for **£25**.
>
> **Contribution per unit = £25 – £5 = £20**
>
> **Break even output = £ 3000 ÷ £20 = 150** So, Harry has to sell **150** T-shirts to **break even**.

Draw a Break Even Chart to show Break Even Point

1) Break even charts plot **costs** and **revenues** against **output**. Businesses use break even charts to see how costs and revenues **vary** with different levels of output.

2) **Output** goes on the **horizontal axis**. The scale needs to let you plot output from 0 to the maximum possible.

3) **Costs and revenue** both go on the vertical axis. Use a scale that lets you plot from 0 to the maximum revenue.

4) Next, plot **fixed** costs. (On the diagram below, fixed costs are the blue horizontal line.)

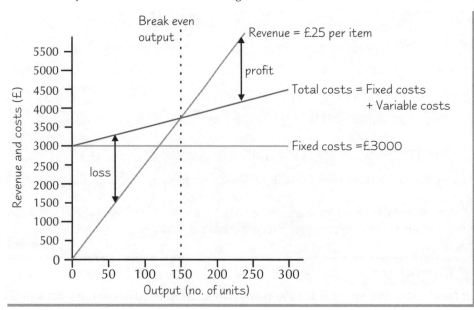

5) **Add** variable costs to fixed costs to get the **total cost**, and plot it on the graph. (The total costs are shown by the purple line, starting at the same point as the fixed costs line.)

6) Next, plot **revenue** on the graph. Revenue is the selling price per item. (It's the green line on the diagram.)

7) The **break even point** is where the **revenue** line crosses the **total costs** line.

Break Even

The **Margin of Safety** is the amount between **Current Output** and **Break Even**

Margin of safety = current output − break even output

OK, back to Harry's T-shirt business again. The diagram on the right shows the margin of safety for Harry's business when his output is 250 T-shirts. If Harry sells **250** T-shirts, the margin of safety is 250 − 150 = **100**.

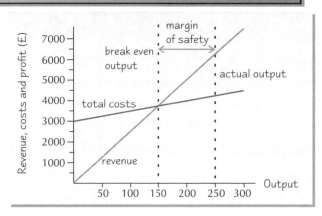

Break even analysis has **Advantages** and **Disadvantages**

Advantages of break even analysis

1) It's **pig easy** to do. If you can plot figures on a graph accurately, you can do break even analysis.
2) It's **quick** — managers can see **break even** and **margin of safety** immediately. This allows managers to take **quick action** to cut costs or increase sales if they need to **increase** their margin of safety.
3) Break even charts let businesses **forecast** how variations in sales will affect **costs**, **revenue** and **profits**.
4) Businesses can use break even analysis to help **persuade** the bank to give them a **loan**.

Disadvantages of break even analysis

1) **Break even analysis assumes that variable costs** always rise steadily. In real life, this isn't always the case. A business can get **discounts** for buying in **bulk** — that means that costs don't go up in direct **proportion** with output. A real life costs line would be a curve that gets flatter as output increases.
2) Break even analysis is nice and simple for a **single product** — but most businesses sell lots of products, so looking at the business as a whole can get a lot more complicated.
3) If the **data** is wrong, then the **results** will be wrong. **Wrong estimates** of costs and revenue will give you the **wrong figure** for break even. For example, **costs** and **selling price** both **rise** over time, which could lead to original estimates becoming less accurate.
4) Break even analysis assumes the business **sells all the products**, without any wastage. But, for example, a restaurant business will end up throwing away food if fewer customers turn up than they're expecting.
5) Break even analysis only tells you how many units you **need** to sell to break even. It **doesn't** tell you how many you're **actually going to sell**.

Practice Questions

Q1 Write down the formula for contribution, and the formula for break even output.
Q2 Write down two advantages and two disadvantages of break even analysis.

Exam Questions

Q1 Bob is deciding whether to set up in business selling fishing equipment. Discuss the value of break even analysis in helping Bob decide whether or not to go ahead with the business. (10 marks)

Q2 Muneer Khan has a small restaurant. The average price per customer per meal is £13. The variable costs of materials and labour per meal are £5. The fixed costs of the restaurant are £1000 per month. Calculate the break even number of customers per month. (4 marks)

Answer on p.102.

Ah, give us a break...

You can either be asked to write about break even analysis, or you can be asked to actually do it. Luckily, it's not hard. The examiners could be sneaky and decide to ask you to evaluate the benefits of break even analysis to a particular firm, instead of getting you to do some nice easy break even sums. So, make sure you're aware of the advantages and disadvantages.

Company Accounts

Accounts show a business how it's doing, in nice facts and figures. They also give accountants something to do.
These pages are for Edexcel and OCR.

Businesses complete **Accounts** once a year

1) Accounting information is presented in a set of standard reports. The three main reports are the **profit and loss account** (see p.48), the **balance sheet** (see p.47) and the **cash flow statement** (which is like the cash flow forecast on p.39, except that it shows **actual** figures instead of **predicted** ones).

2) The **law** says that **limited companies** have to **publish** their financial reports **every year**. They publish reports which are **summaries** of more detailed reports, to stop competitors learning too much about their businesses.

Accounts help managers to make decisions

There are two types of accounting — financial accounting and management accounting.

Financial accounting	Management accounting
Reports are published for use outside the business.	Reports are for use inside the business.
Financial accounting follows rules and regulations.	No regulations are needed.
Records financial transactions up to a specific date.	Forecasts future performance based on past performance.
Includes profit and loss account and balance sheet.	Includes break-even, budgeting and cost/profit centres.

1) Accounts help **business owners** to see how the business is doing. They like to know whether the business is profitable, if it can pay its short term bills, how much money is on loan, and what its assets and liabilities are.

2) **Managers** need accounts to help them make good **business decisions**.

3) All the **stakeholders** in a business (see p.2) can make use of financial information.

4) Banks who **lend** money to businesses like to know how the business is doing. They need to know if the business can pay its bills, how many assets it has, and whether it can turn its assets into cash quickly enough to pay off its debts.

Businesses use **Accounting Principles** when doing their accounts

1) Accounting principles and conventions are an agreed set of rules that businesses use to prepare their accounts.

2) Accounting conventions say that businesses must present data that are a "**true and fair**" reflection of how they're doing — although they do have some freedom to decide how they will **present** this data.

3) They assume that a business will **carry on trading** as usual for the **foreseeable future** unless there's specific **evidence** to say otherwise. This is called the "**going concern**" convention.

4) They assume that the value of assets is stated as their **value to the business** going forward, not their purchase price when new. Assets are **depreciated** (see p.48).

5) Expenditure is classified according to whether it adds value to the business as a **whole (capital expenditure)** or is a necessary expense of **doing business** (**revenue expenditure**).

6) Because accounts are done in a **standard** way, you can **compare** one firm's accounts with another's.

Accounts can be **Misleading**

1) Accounts can be **tweaked** to make things look **better** (or **worse**) than they really are — as long as they still comply with the accounting principles.

2) Businesses do this for several reasons — to **mislead competitors**, to try and pay **less tax** on profits, to present a flattering picture before **asking** for a **loan**, to **increase share price**, or to **boost asset value** before a take-over bid.

3) Businesses can do several rather bad and naughty things to manipulate their data:

- They can **tweak depreciation levels** — saying that assets have lost **more** or **less** value than they really have.
- They can classify **operating expenditure** (an **overhead** on the Profit and Loss Account) as **capital expenditure** (an **asset** on the Balance Sheet).
- They can bring future orders **forward**.
- They can **delay payments** that are due to creditors.
- They can **over-value** non-physical assets like **customer goodwill** or **brand image**.

But remember, accounting principles restrict the extent to which data can be manipulated.

Company Accounts: Balance Sheet

Balance Sheets are lists of Assets and Liabilities

1) Balance sheets are a **snapshot** of a firm's finances at a **fixed point in time**. They show the value of all the **assets** (the things that belong to the business, including cash in the bank) and all the **liabilities** (the money the business owes).

2) Balance sheets also show the value of all the **capital** in the business, and the source of that capital — they show where the money's **come from** as well as what's being **done** with it.

3) Balance sheets have to... **balance**.

Understanding a Balance Sheet

1) **Fixed assets** are assets which are kept for **more than a year**. The value of most fixed assets decreases each year, as they are **used up** or **wear out**. This is **depreciation** — it's measured on the profit and loss account.

2) **Current assets** last **less** then a year. Current assets are listed in increasing order of **liquidity**, from **stock** to **cash**. They keep circulating — cash pays for stock, when stock is sold the business is owed money by **debtors**.

3) **Current liabilities** are **debts** the company owes which need to be paid off within a year.

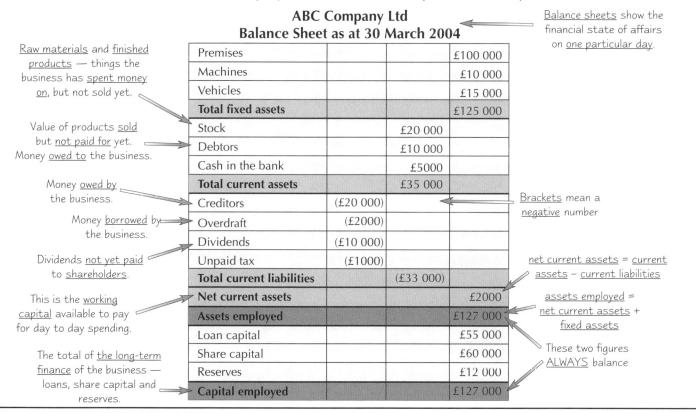

ABC Company Ltd
Balance Sheet as at 30 March 2004

Premises			£100 000
Machines			£10 000
Vehicles			£15 000
Total fixed assets			£125 000
Stock		£20 000	
Debtors		£10 000	
Cash in the bank		£5000	
Total current assets		£35 000	
Creditors	(£20 000)		
Overdraft	(£2000)		
Dividends	(£10 000)		
Unpaid tax	(£1000)		
Total current liabilities		(£33 000)	
Net current assets			£2000
Assets employed			£127 000
Loan capital			£55 000
Share capital			£60 000
Reserves			£12 000
Capital employed			£127 000

Balance sheets show the financial state of affairs on one particular day.

Raw materials and finished products — things the business has spent money on, but not sold yet.

Value of products sold but not paid for yet. Money owed to the business.

Money owed by the business.

Money borrowed by the business.

Dividends not yet paid to shareholders.

This is the working capital available to pay for day to day spending.

The total of the long-term finance of the business — loans, share capital and reserves.

Brackets mean a negative number

net current assets = current assets – current liabilities

assets employed = net current assets + fixed assets

These two figures ALWAYS balance

Practice Questions

Q1 Give three reasons why businesses keep accounts.

Q2 Give three examples of fixed assets and three examples of current assets.

Q3 Which report shows the state of the business on one day only rather than over a defined period?

Exam Questions

Q1 Outline the benefits of using standard accounting practices. (6 marks)

Q2 Construct a balance sheet for a business where fixed assets are worth £200 000, stock £20 000, and debtors £10 000. Within the next 12 months creditors are owed £70 000. Assume the business is financed from reserves and share capital, and that reserves are £100 000. (4 marks)

It's easy to balance on a sheet — sheets are flat... now, pencils on the other hand...

Accounting reports are a starting point for understanding a business. It's important that businesses all do them in pretty much the same way, otherwise you'd never be able to compare two sets of accounts. Make sure you understand what all the technical terms mean and how the figures in the big blue balance sheet add up — and why balance sheets balance.

Company Accounts: Profit and Loss

Page 48 is for AQA, Edexcel and OCR. Page 49 is only for OCR.

Profit and Loss Accounts calculate Profits over a period of Time

1) The profit and loss (P&L) account is really **three** accounts rolled into one.

2) The **trading account** works out **gross profit** — revenue minus direct costs.

3) The **profit and loss account** subtracts overheads to work out **net profit**.

4) The **appropriation account** shows how profits are **distributed** between shareholders or **kept** in the business.

5) P&L accounts are generally drawn up for **a full year** — reporting a shorter period can be **misleading**. For example, High Street retailers can generate **half their annual revenue** in the lead-up to **Christmas** — a profit and loss account ignoring this period won't give anything like an accurate picture of the business.

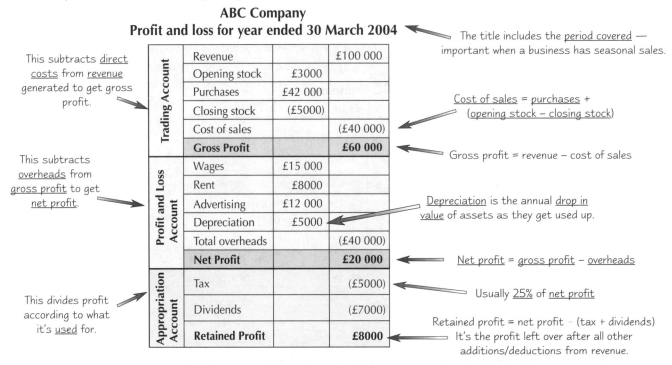

ABC Company
Profit and loss for year ended 30 March 2004

The title includes the period covered — important when a business has seasonal sales.

This subtracts direct costs from revenue generated to get gross profit.

Trading Account		
Revenue		£100 000
Opening stock	£3000	
Purchases	£42 000	
Closing stock	(£5000)	
Cost of sales		(£40 000)
Gross Profit		**£60 000**

Cost of sales = purchases + (opening stock – closing stock)

Gross profit = revenue – cost of sales

This subtracts overheads from gross profit to get net profit.

Profit and Loss Account		
Wages	£15 000	
Rent	£8000	
Advertising	£12 000	
Depreciation	£5000	
Total overheads		(£40 000)
Net Profit		**£20 000**

Depreciation is the annual drop in value of assets as they get used up.

Net profit = gross profit – overheads

This divides profit according to what it's used for.

Appropriation Account		
Tax		(£5000)
Dividends		(£7000)
Retained Profit		**£8000**

Usually 25% of net profit

Retained profit = net profit – (tax + dividends) It's the profit left over after all other additions/deductions from revenue.

Accounts reflect Assets that Depreciate — they Lose Value over Time

1) The **drop in value** of a business asset over time is called **depreciation**.

2) Businesses **depreciate** their assets every year to make sure that their **value** as recorded on the **balance sheet** is a **true reflection** of what the asset is worth to the business. The **amount** of depreciation is recorded on the **profit and loss account** as an **expense**.

3) Building depreciation into each year's accounts **stops** the cost hitting **all at once** when the firm **buys** the asset.

4) The **straight line method** of calculating depreciation splits it equally over the life of an asset. This method is quick and simple, but you need to know how long the asset lasts and how much it's worth when you eventually replace it. The amount an asset is worth when you get rid of it is called the **residual value**.

$$\text{Depreciation per year} = \frac{\text{cost of asset} - \text{residual value}}{\text{useful life of asset}}$$

Example: A piece of machinery costs **£10 000** when new. It's expected to last **8 years**. After 8 years, it's worth **£600**.

$$\text{Depreciation} = \frac{£10\,000 - £600}{8} = £1175$$

5) The **reducing balance method** assumes an asset depreciates by an **equal percentage** of its current worth throughout its life. Most of the asset's value is lost in the **first year**. This method is often more **accurate** but it's also more **complicated** and **time-consuming**.

Example: An asset costs **£20 000** to buy new. It will last for **3 years**. It depreciates at **25%** per year. After **1 year**, it's worth £20 000 × 75% = **£15 000** (so depreciation = **£5000**). After **2 years**, it's worth £15 000 × 75% = **£11 250** (and depreciation = **£3750**). After **3 years**, it's worth £11 250 × 75% = **£8437.50** (depreciation = **£2812.50**).

Investment Analysis

Managers use Profit Information to make Investment Decisions

1) Investors want to invest in businesses that are going to make **lots** and lots of **profit**. They want as much **return** on their investment as possible — they want to **make as much money** as possible.

2) **Senior managers** in a business use **profit information** to decide whether to go ahead with a **project**. They **compare projects** by **payback period** (how long they take to cover their costs) and **accounting rate of return** (how profitable they are). This type of analysis is called an **investment appraisal**.

3) Investors and senior managers both like to keep risks as **low as possible** when things are financially **insecure**.

Payback is the amount of Time it takes to get your Money Back

A business with cash flow problems will want a **quick payback period**. It'll need to get a return on its investment as **quickly** as possible because it **can't afford** to hang around **waiting** for a project to make money.

Accounting Rate of Return compares Profit with Investment

A business that isn't in danger of running out of money will want to do projects with as **high** an **accounting rate of return** as possible.

$$\text{Accounting rate of return} = \frac{\text{average annual profit}}{\text{investment}} \times 100\,\%$$

Here's an example:
Managers are **choosing** between project X and project Y. The predicted **net cash inflow** for each project is in this table.

Year	0	1	2	3	4	5
Project X	(£7m)	£3m	£4m	£4m	£5m	£5m
Project Y	(£6m)	£2m	£3m	£3m	£4m	£4m

Initial investment for project **X** is **£7m**. After 2 years, it'll make £7m. The payback period is **2 years**. Simplicity itself.

Net profit for project X (£m) = 3 + 4 + 4 + 5 + 5 − 7 = **£14m**
Average annual profit for project X = 14 ÷ 5 = **£2.8m**
Accounting rate of return for project X = 2.8 ÷ 7 × 100% = **40%**

Initial investment for project **Y** is **£6m**. After 2 years, the inflow is £5m. It needs £1m more to pay back the investment. The forecast cash inflow for the 3rd year is £3m — so it'll make back the extra million in a third of a year, or 4 months. The total payback period is **2 years 4 months**.

Net profit for project Y (£m) = 2 + 3 + 3 + 4 + 4 − 6 = **£10m**
Average annual profit for project Y = 10 ÷ 5 = **£2m**
Accounting rate of return for project Y = 2 ÷ 6 × 100% = **33.33%**

The managers will choose **project X**, unless they're **daft**. It has a **shorter** payback period, and a **higher** accounting rate of return.

Investment appraisals aren't always so clear-cut. Before making a decision, managers must consider the business's **objectives** (whether it's better to cover costs quickly or make loadsa profit), **and** whether the appraisal is **correct**. Both **payback period** and **accounting rate of return** are only as good as the **data** used to calculate them.

OCR   OCR   OCR

Practice Questions

Q1 What is depreciation?

Q2 A project starts off with £10 000 investment. It brings in £2000 in year 1, £3000 in year 2, £3000 in year 3 and £4000 in year 4. Work out the payback period and accounting rate of return.

Exam Questions

Q1 Construct a profit and loss account for a business where turnover = £24 000, cost of sales = £9000, wages = £3000, other overheads = £4000, tax = 25% of net profit, and dividends = £5000. (6 marks)

Q2 Barry is thinking of opening a fast food franchise. The start-up costs are £35 000 in total. The predicted net cash inflows are £10 000 in year 1, £10 000 in year 2, £15 000 in year 3, £20 000 in year 4, £20 000 in year 5. Calculate the payback period and accounting rate of return. (7 marks)

Answers on p.102.

Learn this — you just might profit from it...

The profit and loss account is fairly easy to understand. You add up sales, take off direct costs, take off overheads and voila, profit. Working out accounting rate of return and payback period can be slightly tricky. It is maths after all. Luckily, it's fairly easy maths — it's only hard until you've practised a few calculations and figured out what's what.

Company Accounts: Ratios

Business managers and investors analyse company accounts to see what state their finances are in.
Welcome to the joys of Ratio Analysis. **These two pages are just for Edexcel.**

Profitability Ratios — how much **Profit** in relation to **Turnover** and **Capital**

1) **Gross** and **net profit margins** express profit as a percentage of revenue.
Gross margin is higher because it doesn't include overheads.

$$\text{Gross profit margin} = \frac{\text{gross profit}}{\text{revenue}} \times 100\,\%$$

$$\text{Net profit margin} = \frac{\text{net profit}}{\text{revenue}} \times 100\,\%$$

2) High percentages are best, but what's good or bad varies between industries. A **net profit margin** of **11%** would be considered **good** for a **supermarket** but **poor** for a **computer software firm** with new patented technology. Comparing ratios to industry averages is a way of analysing whether profit margins are good.

3) **Return on capital employed** measures profits as a percentage of **capital invested** in the business. If it falls **below** the current **bank interest rate** the business would get a **better return** on its money by putting it in a **bank**.

$$\text{Return on capital employed} = \frac{\text{net profit}}{\text{capital employed}} \times 100\,\%$$

Liquidity Ratios — how much money is available to **Pay** the **Bills**

1) A firm without enough **working capital** is suffering from poor **liquidity**. It might have the assets, but it can't **use** them to **pay** for things here and now.

2) A business which doesn't have enough current assets to pay their liabilities when they become due is **insolvent** — they can't pay their bills. They either have to generate the money very quickly, or give up and **cease trading**.

3) **Working capital** and **liquidity** can be **improved** by reducing stock, speeding up collection of debts owed to the business, or slowing down payments to creditors (e.g. suppliers).

4) The **liquidity** of an asset is how easily it can be turned into **cash** and used to **buy** things. **Cash** is **very** liquid, **fixed assets** such as **factories** are **not liquid**, stock and money owed by creditors are in between.

5) There are **two** liquidity ratios you need to know — the **acid test ratio** and **current ratio**.

1) The **acid test ratio** compares **current assets (excluding stock)** to current liabilities. It shows how much of what a business owes in the short-term is covered by its current assets. It doesn't include stock, because it isn't always easy to sell stock in time to pay off debts.

$$\text{acid test ratio} = \frac{\text{current assets} - \text{stock}}{\text{current liabilities}} \quad \text{(written as a ratio } x\text{:1)} \qquad \text{for example: } \frac{£30\,000}{£32\,000} = 0.9375\text{:1}$$

2) A ratio of 1:1 is ideal — it shows **both** amounts are the **same**. A value much **more** than this means the business has **money lying around** that they could use more profitably if they invested it elsewhere. A ratio of less than 1:1 means the business doesn't have **enough** current assets to **pay its bills.** A ratio of 0.8:1 shows a firm has only 80p of current assets for every £1 of current liabilities it owes. Not good....

All the data needed to calculate current ratio and acid test ratio are found on the balance sheet.

1) **Current ratio** compares **current assets (including stock)** to current liabilities. It's also called the **working capital** ratio.

$$\text{current ratio} = \frac{\text{current assets}}{\text{current liabilities}} \quad \text{(expressed as a ratio } x\text{:1)}$$

2) In reality, the business might not be **able** to **sell off** all its stock. It would also need **additional capital** to **replace** stocks. So, the current ratio should be **higher** than 1:1 to take account of this. A ratio of between 1.5:1 and 2:1 is considered about right.

3) A value much below 1.5:1 suggests a **liquidity problem** and difficulty meeting current liabilities. This is called **overtrading**.

Company Accounts: Ratios

How a business is financed will **Affect Performance**

1) **Gearing** shows the **percentage** of a business's capital that comes from **long-term loans** (debt) rather than **share capital** or **reserves** (equity).

$$\text{Gearing} = \frac{\text{long-term loans}}{\text{capital employed}} \times 100 \%$$

Gearing is calculated using information from the lower half of a balance sheet — the part that shows where the money comes from.

2) A gearing **above 50%** shows a business is **high-geared**, **below 50%** shows it is **low-geared**.

3) **High gearing** can cause problems with **decision-making** — banks loaning capital have a larger stake in the business than the shareholders, so they might want a say in how the business is run.

4) **High gearing** can also cause **cash flow problems** — the business is likely to have large monthly loan repayments that use up some of the liquid assets, and reduce profits available for investing back into the business. Also, loan repayments can turn into a big burden if interest rates rise.

5) When **interest rates** are **low**, high gearing can be a **good** thing. Loan repayments are cheap — and investing additional capital can generate additional **profits** that are **bigger** than the loan repayments.

When the cost of borrowing is low, it pays to borrow.

6) **Low gearing** might mean the business isn't very **ambitious**, and isn't taking enough **risks**. Managers would be right to borrow lots of capital if it meant they could **make the most** of a business **opportunity** before their competitors got a look-in.

Ratios **Aren't** the **Be-all** and **End-all** of decision-making

1) Ratios ignore things that you can't express in figures — factors such as the quality of **leadership** and staff **motivation**. Ratios ignore **non-financial assets** like the value of a brand, patents, trademarks and customer goodwill.

2) Ratios are based on **accounting data** that might contain **errors**.

3) Ratios use **historical** data — figures from the past year, or from previous years. This might not always be a good indication of **future** performance, especially in **fast-changing markets**.

4) Managers should use non-financial information **alongside** ratios to make sure they make the **best decisions**.

Kat's leaf filing business had a terrible current ratio, but she just didn't care.

Practice Questions

Q1 State the formulae for the "acid test" and "return on capital employed" ratios.

Q2 What is the ideal figure for the acid test ratio?

Q3 State four drawbacks of basing decision-making purely on ratio analysis.

Q4 What is meant by the term 'insolvent'?

Answer to part (a) on p.102.

Exam Question

Q1 A business has £1200 in stock and is owed £800 by debtors. It owes £400 to suppliers, £400 in tax and £100 in loan interest to the bank. Its turnover is £16 000 and net profit is £4000.
   (a) Work out: i) the acid test ratio (2 marks)
   ii) the current ratio. (2 marks)
   iii) the net profit margin. (2 marks)
   (b) What additional information might you want before deciding if these ratios were good or bad? (6 marks)

Think of a number... divide it by sales turnover...subtract capital

Ratios are very useful for spotting financial problems in a business. You can use ratios to tell you if a business is making enough profit, if it has enough working capital, and if it's in too much debt. Ratios aren't everything though, they're just a quick and simple tool. There's a lot more information that you need to say if a business is really doing well.

Human Resources

These pages tell you how businesses figure out their staff needs. **These two pages are for AQA and OCR only.**

Human Resource Management (HRM) *looks after all workers in a business*

Human Resource Management (HRM) looks after everyone from **senior managers** to **part-time unskilled workers**. The main function of Human Resources is to make sure that the business has the **right number of employees** and that they're of the **right quality** in terms of **qualifications and skills**.

HRM departments have a **different role** to traditional **personnel** departments:

Traditional Personnel Department	A Human Resources (HRM) Department
Personnel is a **support department**. It's responsible for **recruitment**, **training**, **welfare** and **termination** of staff.	The HRM department has a **higher status** — it's important in the **corporate planning and strategy** of a business.
Personnel gets staff trained to meet the aims of the business — this is called **narrow support**.	HRM supports the **needs and ambitions** of staff to keep them contributing to the business — this is **broad support**.
Only the personnel department is responsible for staff **welfare**.	Staff welfare isn't centralised to the HRM department — it's seen as the responsibility of **all managers**.
Personnel recruits and trains for **specific jobs**.	HRM tries to recognise each employee as an **individual** with potential. Staff aren't tied to one fixed job role.
Staff are recruited and trained to **slot into the hierarchy** of the business. This means the hierarchy gets reinforced.	All employees share the **same vision** and common aims so the hierarchy becomes **less important**.

Human Resource Management *keeps a business* Flexible

Businesses need to be **flexible** enough to react in a competitive and changing environment. Change comes from consumer demand, new technology and new laws. **Competitors** are constantly joining and leaving the market.

1) The HRM department has to make sure the **number** and **quality** of the staff keeps up with changing demands.

2) The HRM department also needs to set up a **performance management system** to check that human resources are always being used to maximum efficiency.

Human Resources Planning *predicts* How Many Workers *are needed*

1) Human Resources plans for a firm's future staffing needs — **how many workers** will be needed and what kind of workforce will be needed — **skilled/unskilled**, **full-time/part-time**.

2) HRM plans how to **recruit** staff — where to advertise, how to interview, etc.

3) Human Resources also decides how to treat staff while they're working for the business — how to **use their skills**, how to **retain** them, how to **train** and **reward** them, and eventually how to **terminate** their employment.

4) **Human Resources strategies** can be **short-term** (e.g. recruiting part-time staff for Christmas sales in retailing) or **long-term** (e.g. anticipating growth or a change in production techniques).

Human Resources *assess* Supply *and* Demand *of workers*

HRM departments in a business assess **demand for workers** in several ways:

1) HRM departments ask **other experienced managers** for their **opinions** and **advice**.

2) **Past statistics** (backdata) are used to see if employee numbers have **risen**, **fallen** or **stayed the same**.

3) An increase or decrease in **demand for product** means an increase or decrease in **need for workers**.

4) Human Resources analyse the **current staff details** to see how many are likely to **leave** or **retire** in the near future.

5) The introduction of **new techniques** (e.g. automation) will alter the number of workers needed.

6) Businesses do an **internal stocktake**. They look at all the **jobs** in the organisation — what each job entails and what sort of **qualities** and **skills** are needed. They then see whether current staff **match** these requirements.

Human Resources also need to assess the potential **supply** of **new workers**:

1) They check the **level of unemployment** in the area to find out how many people are looking for work.

2) **Local infrastructure** is important — good housing, transport and schools can **tempt** people to the area.

3) Businesses see how many **school and college leavers** are seeking employment locally.

4) Businesses see if **competitors** are recruiting a similar workforce — if there'll be **competition** for workers.

Human Resources

Achieving labour targets — *Expanding the Workforce*

If a business thinks they need to **expand**, they have to decide whether to recruit
externally (from outside) or **internally** (by training and promoting current employees).

As part of this process, businesses try to calculate the current **staff turnover**. This is how many staff
on average leave the business for one reason or another over, say, a year. To do this, they use this **formula**:

$$\frac{\text{Number of staff leaving over the period}}{\text{Average number of staff employed}} \times 100 = \text{Staff turnover \%}$$

Example: On average, a business employs 500 staff and on average 25 leave each year.
The **average staff turnover** would be: $25 \div 500 \times 100 = 5\%$

How the Human Resources department decides to **recruit** depends on the **kind of business**, the **size of
the business** and the **kind of workers** needed. There's **more** about recruitment on the next few pages.

Achieving labour targets — *Reducing the Workforce*

Reducing the size of the workforce is **much harder** than expanding the workforce.

1) The **least painful** method is through **natural wastage** — this is where staff
    leave of their own accord by leaving for **other work** or through **retirement**.

2) If natural wastage isn't enough a firm may offer its older workers
    early retirement — a **financial encouragement** to retire early.

3) A business may need to make some of its workers **redundant** — they have to
    leave as their job won't exist any more. Under the **Employment Rights Act
    (1996)**, workers who've been with a business for a **year** have the right to
    severance pay (the actual amount depends on the length of service and the
    wage at the time of redundancy). Businesses **can't re-advertise** a redundant
    job — redundancy means the **job doesn't exist any more.**

4) The **Employment Protection Act (1978)** protects workers against **unfair
    dismissal**. They can only legally be sacked if they're **incompetent**,
    unable to perform the role they're in, or guilty of **gross misconduct**.

5) Workers who have been **unfairly dismissed** or **unfairly made redundant** can
    appeal to an **employment tribunal**.

Practice Questions

Q1   A business employs 800 people on average, and on average 40 people leave each year.
     Calculate their staff turnover.

Q2   Give four pieces of information a business might use to help estimate the demand for labour in the future.

Q3   Describe three methods a HRM department could use to measure the potential supply of labour in their area.

Exam Questions

Q1   The Managing Director of a company believes that the upturn in the national economy will boost sales.
     He asks the head of Human Resources to prepare a report assessing the need to increase the labour force
     and indicating in general how to meet this need. Suggest what the report should contain, giving reasons
     for your suggestions.   (14 marks)

Q2   Identify and briefly explain the differences between a HRM department
     and a traditional Personnel department.   (8 marks)

I'm thinking of taking on an assistant to help me write these tips...

*These pages really aren't that bad to learn. Most of the stuff about Human Resource Management is common sense.
Obviously, a business would need to make sure it was employing the right number of people to do the work, and that
they all had the right qualifications and training.*

Workers

The main function of the HRM department is to make sure that the business recruits the right number of employees with the right qualities in terms of skills, knowledge and potential. **These pages are for AQA and OCR.**

The **Human Resources Cycle**

| 1) Selection | 2) Induction | 3) Training | 4) Performance | 5) Appraisal | 6) Development | 7) Departure |

1) **Selection** means recruiting the most **suitable applicant**.

2) **Induction** means introducing the new recruit to the workings of the organisation and to relevant **colleagues**.

3) **Training** is the process of giving the new employee the appropriate **knowledge** and **skills** to function efficiently.

4) **Performance** is the part where the employee actually does their **tasks** and meets **targets**.

5) **Appraisal** looks at the performance and effectiveness of the employee over a period of time. It gives **feedback** and sorts out support and further training if the worker needs it.

6) **Development** supports the employee. It includes promotion or transfer to other areas, to gain experience.

7) **Departure** is the **end** of the job. **Everyone** comes to the end of a job eventually. This can happen through **retirement** or **promotion** — or in less satisfactory situations, **redundancy** or **dismissal**.

Businesses can recruit **Internally** or **Externally**

Internal recruitment = from people who **already** work for the business. **External recruitment** = from the big wide world.

Advantages of internal recruitment	1) Managers **know** the internal candidates. 2) Internal candidates **know the business** and its objectives. 3) It's a **shorter** and **less expensive** process than external recruitment. 4) It **motivates** workers by encouraging them to go for promotion.
Disadvantages of internal recruitment	1) Internal promotion leaves **another vacancy** to be filled. 2) It can cause **resentment** among colleagues who aren't selected.
Advantages of external recruitment	1) External recruits bring in **fresh new ideas**. 2) External recruits bring **experience** from other organisations. 3) There's a larger pool of applicants to **choose** from.
Disadvantages of external recruitment	1) Managers **don't know** the applicant. 2) It's usually a **long** and **expensive** process. 3) External recruits usually need a longer **induction** process.

Businesses **advertise** vacancies to external applicants in national newspapers, specialist trade magazines, local newspapers and through specialist employment agencies or job centres. **Where** they advertise the job depends on the **type** of job, the **size** of the organisation and **where** the organisation operates.

Selection — getting the **Right People** for the job

It's obviously important to get the best possible candidate for a job. To have the best chance of getting the best people, the HR department **analyses** the vacancy and draws up a **job description** and a **person specification**.

1) The **job description** lists the tasks and responsibilities the person appointed will be expected to carry out. It may also state the job title, the location, the nature of the business and other details like salary and conditions (e.g. holiday entitlement, pension arrangements and so on).

2) The **person specification** outlines the ideal profile of the person needed to match the job description. It describes their **qualifications**, experience, interests and **personality**. It's important to know whether the candidate will fit into the **culture** and **atmosphere** of the business, as well as knowing whether they've got a GNVQ in Tourism, or if they can do SQL programming.

Methods of selection include **Interviews** and **Tests**

1) **Interviews** are the most common way of choosing candidates. Candidates can be interviewed **one-to-one** or by a **panel** of interviewers. Phone interviews are thought to be less effective than **face-to-face** interviews.

2) Some organisations use **assessment centres** to help them **test** candidates. Tests include **psychometric** testing which assesses personality fit, **aptitude** tests which find out how good the candidate is at job tasks, and **group exercises** which show how candidates interact with other people in various situations.

Workers

Employment Contracts set out the Terms of the Job

1) Once a successful candidate gets the job, they sign a contract of employment — a **legally binding document** which outlines the **terms** and **conditions** of the person's job.

2) The contract states whether the job is part-time or full-time, temporary or permanent. It quotes the **salary** or rate of pay, the **hours**, the holiday entitlement, benefits, the period of **notice** required as well as the **disciplinary** and grievance procedures.

3) The rights and responsibilities of employers and employees are set out in **law**, and contracts of employment must not breach them.

Employees need Training and Development

1) The **first day** or so on the job is usually spent learning the workings of the business, the health and safety issues and meeting key personnel. This is the **induction** part of the human resources cycle.

2) Most new employees need some training — either to learn **new skills** or **improve** and **update** existing skills.

3) Training can be done **off the job** — e.g. studying part time at a local **college**, a short one or two day **course** at a business training centre or **studying at home** for a professional qualification.

4) Training can be done **on the job** — i.e. in the workplace.

On the job training can take several forms: *This is rather endearingly called "sitting next to Nellie".*

1) The **traditional** way is to sit the new trainee next to an **experienced worker**. The newbie watches and learns from the experienced worker, and the experienced worker is there to answer any questions about the job.

2) **Mentoring** is where the new employee is supervised by an experienced worker who acts as **tutor** and guru.

3) **Coaching** is where the new trainee is given **specialised training**, e.g. how to operate a particular machine.

4) **Job rotation** is where the new person **moves around** the organisation and experiences **different jobs**.

Businesses should **evaluate** their training to see how it's **working**, using clear, measurable training objectives. Managers should be able to compare training costs with the financial gains in overall performance.

Well-trained staff are important in a business, but sometimes businesses might not actually want to be the **best** at training staff. They worry that **competitors** will "**poach**" the staff they've trained. Taken to extremes, this would result in "market failure" — **no training** being done, and the labour market grinding to a halt.

Some organisations do **employee development** as well as training:

1) Whereas training focuses on **particular skills**, development programmes try to help employees learn and improve **broader** skills, and **get ahead** in the organisation.

2) The idea is that the organisation will benefit from a more **fulfilled** and **motivated** employee.

Practice Questions

Q1 Outline one advantage and one disadvantage of both internal recruitment and external recruitment.

Q2 Briefly explain the terms "job description" and "person specification".

Q3 Explain the difference between on-the-job training and off-the-job training.

Q4 List and describe three methods of on-the-job training.

Exam Questions

Q1 A major London hotel wants to recruit an experienced accountant. Outline the procedures they may follow in the recruitment process. (9 marks)

Q2 Produce a brief report summarising the advantages and disadvantages of internal and external recruitment for a retail organisation with 200 stores nationwide. (15 marks)

Interviews are a nightmare for everyone...

Reading this page, I don't know which is worse — being interviewed for a job, or having to interview someone else for a job, and then deciding whether to offer it to them or not. Recruitment can be a long and drawn-out process. It's important to get it right, especially if you're planning on paying the new person a lot of money to do a crucial job.

Business Structures

The structure of a business depends on its size, its geographical distribution, the kind of product or service it offers and the history and culture of the organisation. ***These two pages are for AQA, OCR and Edexcel.***

Structure and Hierarchy are shown by an Organisational Chart

1) The traditional business structure is a series of levels, where each level has responsibility and authority over the levels below. This is called a **hierarchy**.

2) An **organisational chart** sets out who has **authority** to make decisions and the **responsibility** for making them.

3) It shows who individual employees are **accountable** to — who is directly **above** them in the hierarchy.

4) It shows who employees are **responsible** for — who is directly **below** them in the hierarchy.

5) The chart also shows how the organisation is divided up. It can be divided by **function**, e.g. into a production department, a marketing department etc., or it can be divided by **product** or **geographical area**.

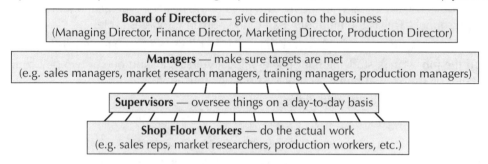

Board of Directors — give direction to the business
(Managing Director, Finance Director, Marketing Director, Production Director)

Managers — make sure targets are met
(e.g. sales managers, market research managers, training managers, production managers)

Supervisors — oversee things on a day-to-day basis

Shop Floor Workers — do the actual work
(e.g. sales reps, market researchers, production workers, etc.)

Structures can be "Tall" or "Flat"

1) Organisations with **lots of levels** in their hierarchy are called "**tall**". They have a large number of people between the top and the bottom. Tall structures have a long **chain of command**. The chain of command is the path of **communication** and **authority** up and down the hierarchy.

2) If the structure is **too tall**, it affects **communication**. Messages take a **long time** to get from one end of the chain of command to the other, and they can get **garbled** on the way. **Decisions** take a long time to make, and there's a lot of **paperwork** to deal with.

3) "**Flat**" organisations only have a few levels in the hierarchy.

4) If the structure is **too flat**, then managers can get **overwhelmed** by too many people reporting to them.

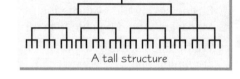

A tall structure

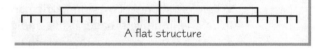

A flat structure

Structures can have broad or narrow Spans of Control

1) Managers in flat organisational structures have wide **spans of control**. This means they have a lot of workers answering to them.

2) Managers in tall structures have **narrower** spans of control — they aren't responsible for as many people. This allows them to **monitor** their subordinates **more closely**.

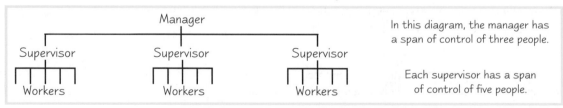

In this diagram, the manager has a span of control of three people.

Each supervisor has a span of control of five people.

3) If the span of control is **too broad**, managers can find it hard to manage **effectively**.

4) If the span of control is **too narrow**, workers can become **demotivated** — they may feel that they're being **micromanaged** (over-managed) by interfering bosses.

5) **Traditionally**, business experts thought it would be hard for a manager to keep a close eye on workers when the span of control is bigger than about 6 people. But if the workers are all doing the **same routine task**, they don't need as much close supervision — so a span of control of 10-12 people is fine.

Business Structures

Delayering *removes layers of hierarchy*

1) **Delayering** is when a business **removes** a layer of the hierarchy from its organisational structure — usually a layer of managers from somewhere in the **middle** of the hierarchy.

2) Delayering helps to **lower costs**. Cutting management jobs can save a lot of money in salaries.

3) After delayering, you get a **flatter** structure with **broader** spans of control. It's worth being careful not to **overdo** it. Managers can end up **stressed** and overworked with **huge** spans of control.

4) Delayering can give junior employees **enhanced roles** with more responsibility.

5) Some businesses use delayering as an **excuse** to cut jobs.

Centralised Structures *keep* Authority *for decisions at the* Top

In an organisation where decision-making is **centralised**, all decisions are made by **one person**, or one committee of **senior managers** right at the **top** of the business.

Advantages of Centralisation	Disadvantages of Centralisation
Business leaders tend to have plenty of **experience**.	Not many people are **expert** enough in **all aspects** of the business.
Managers get an **overview** of the whole business.	Excluding employees from decision making can be **demotivating**.
Senior managers understand **central** budgeting restrictions and can make decisions to save the **whole business** money.	Decisions can take a **long time**. The organisation reacts **slowly** to change, and can end up a couple of steps behind its competitors.

Decentralised Structures *share out the* Authority *to make decisions*

1) Decentralisation **shares out authority** to more **junior** employees.

2) Giving responsibility for decision-making to people below you is called **delegation**. There's more about delegation on p.63.

3) **National** and **multinational** organisations **decentralise** decision-making and delegate power to **regional** managers.

Advantages of Decentralisation	Disadvantages of Decentralisation
Involvement in decision-making **motivates** employees.	Subordinates may not have enough **experience** to make decisions.
Employees can use **expert knowledge** of their sector.	**Inconsistencies** may develop between sectors in a business.
Decisions can be made more **quickly** without having to ask senior managers.	Junior employees may not be able to see the **overall situation** and **needs** of an organisation.

Practice Questions

Q1 Why might a flat structure be popular with junior employees in a business?

Q2 What is meant by "span of control"?

Q3 What is "delayering"? Give one reason why a business might delayer.

Q4 Give two advantages of a centralised decision-making structure.

Exam Questions

Q1 A firm of management consultants have advised Douglas McLeod to delayer and flatten the structure of his business.
(a) What's meant by flattening the structure of the business? (2 marks)
(b) Discuss the factors that Douglas should think about before starting to delayer. (10 marks)

Q2 To what extent is a wide span of control desirable for a manager in a business? (10 marks)

Delayering — isn't that taking off your cardigan when it's warm...

Delayering can be a great way of simplifying things and saving money — if your middle managers are a bunch of useless David Brent types, getting rid of them is the kindest thing to do, really. Both tall and flat structures have pros and cons — learn them in case you get asked to evaluate a particular kind of business structure.

Business Structures

All businesses have a structure of some sort, no matter how big or small they are, how they're owned, or what kind of product or service they sell. **These pages are for Edexcel and AQA.**

A *Functional Structure* divides a business into *Departments*

1) Everyone can see who's responsible for the different aspects of the business.

2) Functional structures are also called **formal**, or **traditional** structures.

3) Functional structures are **tall**, and they usually have **narrow** spans of control.

4) Formal functional organisations are centralised.

See p.56 for flat and tall structures and spans of control.

Disadvantages of a functional structure:

1) Departments **compete** with each other for resources, and to get in the managing director's good books.

2) Large firms with a functional structure have a **long chain of command** — which **slows down** decision-making.

3) **Communication** between departments can be poor.

A *Matrix Structure* is a team of *Specialists* from *Different Departments*

1) A **matrix** is a group of **specialist employees** who are brought together as a **team**, usually to complete a **specific project**. For example, a manufacturer planning to introduce a new product can set up a development team consisting of specialists from the design, production, marketing and finance departments.

2) A matrix structure combines a **vertical chain of command** with **horizontal links** between team members.

3) The matrix structure gives teams a sense of **identity**. Team members have a sense of **responsibility to the team** which is a positive **motivating** factor. Doing varied tasks in a matrix team is also motivating.

4) Teams in matrix structures focus on the project they're doing.

5) New project teams can be formed when needed, which helps the organisation respond to customer needs.

Disadvantages of a matrix structure:

1) Special projects may be **expensive** to set up and maintain.

2) Team members may have the burden of **dual responsibility** — for the special project and for their **normal** role in the organisation.

3) It can be difficult to try and **coordinate** specialists from **different areas** of an organisation.

Jean-Claude was seized by the sudden terrifying realisation that he had <u>absolutely no idea</u> who his boss was.

Small Businesses usually have an *Entrepreneurial Structure*

1) With an entrepreneurial structure, **one person** makes all the decisions.

2) This system has its benefits. Decisions can be made **quickly** because the boss doesn't need to **consult** anyone or get anyone's **approval**. Also, it's clear to everyone who makes the decisions, and who has the power. If the owner is making the decisions, they will work hard to make sure they're the right ones for their business.

3) However, there is also a downside. Employees may be **demotivated** if they feel completely excluded from the decision-making process, and if the entrepreneur is **away** from the business for a while, other workers may feel **reluctant** to make decisions.

4) When a business **expands**, the boss will probably need to start involving **other people** in decision-making.

Large Manufacturers have a *Product-Based Structure*

For example, Unilever manufactures spreads, skincare items, tea, soups, washing powder, toothpaste, ice cream and frozen foods. It has structured its organisation into two sectors — Food, and Home/Personal Care.

1) A product-based structure allows managers to make decisions that are **relevant** to each product division.

2) Each division operates as its own **profit centre** (see p.36). This lets senior management compare the successes of each product group, which can generate **competition**.

3) Competition between sectors can be **healthy**, or it can be **negative**.

4) If each product division has its own internal structure, there may be **unnecessary duplication** — e.g. market research or finance could be **shared** between divisions.

Business Structures

National and International organisations have a Geographical Structure

1) Some large organisations with national or international networks (e.g. banks and supermarkets) have a structure based on regional or country links.

2) Spreading management out between regions makes day-to-day control **easier**. Regional managers are better equipped to deal with **regional changes** in demand.

3) The **regional management** can build up **specialist knowledge** of their particular market.

4) Senior managers can compare the **profitability** of regions, which can generate **competition** between regions.

5) However, there may be a wasteful **duplication** of **resources** between regions.

6) Also, regional managers can end up with local policies which **don't fit** into the overall objectives of the business.

Businesses can base Part of their Structure on Market Segmentation

1) Most large organisations divide their market into **segments** based on gender, age, income, social class, etc. (see p.11).

2) It's **unusual** for the **whole** structure of a business to be based on market segmentation, but there are often people in the business with **specific responsibility** for certain market segments.

3) Senior managers can treat each segment as a **cost and profit centre** (see p.36).

4) It can be **complicated** to coordinate things between managers responsible for particular market segments and managers with **general responsibility** for production, human resources, etc.

There's a Relationship between Culture and Structure

The **culture** of an organisation is how the individual people in the organisation actually perform within their roles, and how they relate to each other. There are several styles of business culture:

1) The **power culture** is where everyone relates to a strong central leader. This is often seen in an **entrepreneurial structure** or in larger organisations where there's a clear leader — e.g. Richard Branson and Virgin Group.

2) In the **role culture**, employees have **clearly defined roles** in an obvious chain of command. There are **set procedures** to follow. This culture seems to go with a **hierarchical** structure, and it's the most **common** one in business.

3) The **task culture** relates closely to the **matrix structure**. It's based on a team working together to complete a specific project. It doesn't need a formal hierarchy.

4) The **person culture** hardly seems to have any formal structure or central leader. Individuals have a lot of freedom within the organisation. The person culture tends to be limited to **creative** organisations such as the **entertainment** industry.

Practice Questions

Q1   Give two advantages and two disadvantages of a matrix structure.

Q2   What advantages are there for a business basing its structure on market segmentation?

Q3   What sort of business might use a geographical structure?
Identify one advantage and one disadvantage of this type of structure.

Exam Questions

Q1   Many small businesses have what has been described as an entrepreneurial structure.
Explain what is meant by this term and identify the strengths and weaknesses of such a structure.   (15 marks)

Q2   Explain the relationship between the formal structure of a business and its culture.
Illustrate your answer by describing two identifiable styles of culture.   (15 marks)

Zzzzzzzzzzzzzzz...

*It's boring isn't it. Still, these poor old businesses have to organise themselves in some way, I suppose. Being able to write clear answers about why a business might have a particular kind of organisation can get you good marks. So it's worth learning all of this about functional, matrix, geographical, product and segment-based structures. Even though it **is** boring.*

Management Styles

The term "management" basically means "getting things done" — usually through influencing people.
These pages are for Edexcel, OCR and AQA.

Managers often need to be Leaders as well

1) Managers **set objectives** for their department, and for the people under them.

2) Managers **organise resources** to get the job done and **achieve** their objectives.

3) Leaders **motivate** people. They **inspire** people to do things which they wouldn't do otherwise.

4) Managers who are good leaders can **persuade** people that the decisions that they make and the objectives they set are the **best** ones.

You could say that bosses get results from their employees by telling them what to do, whereas leaders get results through their employees by inspiring and supporting them.

Leaders need good Leadership Qualities

Leaders tend to have a few **important characteristics** in common:

1) Leaders are **good at analysis**, and they can easily **spot a problem** and see potential **solutions**.

2) They **get on with people** at all levels and they're excellent **communicators**.

3) Leaders believe in their own **abilities**, but they can also identify their **weaknesses**.

4) Leaders have excellent **organisational** skills.

5) Their solutions to problems and their methods are **creative** and **imaginative**.

6) Leaders can act **strongly** and **decisively** when they need to.

There are various different Management Styles

① The **Authoritarian** or **Autocratic** style — the **manager makes decisions** on his or her own. They identify the objectives of the business and say how they're going to be achieved. This style is useful when dealing with lots of **unskilled** workers, and in crisis management. It requires lots of **supervision** and monitoring — workers can't make their own decisions. An authoritarian style can **demotivate** able and intelligent workers.

② *AQA and Edexcel — AQA and Edexcel*
The **Paternalistic** (fatherly) style is a softer form of the autocratic style. The manager makes the decisions after **consultation** with others. They **explain** their decisions to the workers in an attempt to **persuade** the employees that such decisions are in everyone's interest. Paternalistic managers think that getting **involved** and caring about human relations is a **positive motivator**.
AQA and Edexcel — AQA and Edexcel

③ The **Democratic** style — the manager encourages the workforce to **participate** in the decision making process. They **discuss** issues with workers, **delegate responsibility** and **listen** to advice. Democratic leaders have to be good communicators, and their organisations have to be good at dealing with a lot of **to-and-fro communication**. This management style shows managers have a lot of confidence in the workforce — which leads to increased employee **motivation**. It also takes some of the **weight** of decision-making off the manager.

④ *OCR and Edexcel — OCR and Edexcel*
The **Laissez-faire** style is a weak form of leadership. **Management rarely interferes** in the running of the business and the workforce is left to get on with trying to achieve the objectives of the business with minimal input and control from the top. This **hands-off** style of leadership might be appropriate for a small, highly motivated team of **able** workers. For workers who need guidance, it'd be a bit of a disaster.
OCR and Edexcel — OCR and Edexcel

Various Factors affect which Management Style is most Appropriate

1) The way the organisation's been run in the past affects the **expectations** of the workforce, which affects how they might respond to leadership.

2) A **large**, **unskilled** workforce suits an **authoritarian** leadership style, whereas a **small**, **educated** workforce suits a **democratic** approach better.

3) **Urgent** tasks need different management and leadership to **routine** tasks.

The best leaders are the ones who can adapt their style to suit the situation. It's hard to adapt like that, and most leaders have their own natural style that they're happiest with.

Management Styles

McGregor's *Theory X* and *Theory Y* of management — are workers lazy?

1) **Theory X** managers think that workers are only motivated by **money**. They think workers are **essentially lazy** and need constant **supervision** because they're only inclined to do the **minimum** amount of work, and have no desire to get involved in decision-making.

2) **Theory Y** managers believe workers can be **trusted**, are capable of **organising** themselves, can act **responsibly** and can **enjoy** their work — as long as they're **motivated**.

McGregor thought **most** managers were Theory X managers. McGregor went along with Theory Y himself.

Businesses can *Change Aspects* of their *Leadership Style*

AQA

The Traditional Relationship between Managers and Workers — Them and Us

1) Traditionally, management and workers had totally different working conditions. For example, **managers** were paid a **yearly salary**, but workers were paid by the **hour** — workers had to clock in and out, whereas managers didn't. Managers and workers even had different **canteen** facilities and different **toilets**.

2) These contrasting conditions were a major **barrier** to **motivation**, so many businesses tried to move away from the traditional "them and us" divide.

Teamworking and Single Status Initiatives Changed Things

1) Instead of doing the same task on a production line over and over again, workers can be organised into **teams** which are **collectively responsible** for getting a big task or process done (see cell production, p.75).

2) Teamworking **delegates** responsibility to teams and **empowers** team members — teams can **organise themselves** in terms of production and quality control. **Quality circles** are teams responsible for quality improvements throughout an organisation (see p.79).

3) Good teamworking needs team members to be **multi-skilled** — so lots of **training** is on the cards.

4) One **problem** is that teams may set themselves objectives that don't match the objectives of the business.

5) **Single status** initiatives are an attempt to break down the barriers between management and workers by deliberately having the **same working conditions** for everyone, e.g. all employees have equal catering and car-parking facilities. In some organisations, all employees wear a similar uniform.

6) Single status sometimes goes **together** with a move towards teamworking, especially in the Japanese manufacturing firms that pioneered new management styles.

AQA — AQA — AQA

Practice Questions

Q1 Give a reason why managers should also be good leaders.

Q2 Identify and explain three types of leadership style.

Q3 Outline two features of McGregor's Theory X and two features of his Theory Y.

Q4 What are single status initiatives? How can they help worker motivation?

Exam Questions

Q1 Fernanda Dos Santos has just been appointed as Managing Director of Sylvan Shoes Ltd. The workforce is mostly skilled, with a low labour turnover. Discuss the various factors that might influence Fernanda's choice of leadership style. (10 marks)

Q2 C&D Tiles has changed its organisation in response to low efficiency. The old style of working had strict divisions between workers in different departments. The new style of working divides everyone into flexible teams.
(a) C&D Tiles spent money on training when they brought in the new arrangements. Why was this? (5 marks)
(b) Outline the skills that a leader of one of the new teams would need. (6 marks)
(c) Discuss the possible benefits to C&D Tiles of adopting this new, more democratic style of leadership. (11 marks)

I prefer the Queen of Hearts style myself — OFF WITH THEIR HEADS...

Although all managers are different, their methods can be categorised into three or four different styles of management. The basic styles of leadership suit different situations and different kinds of worker. Managers try to mould their style of leadership to suit problems and personalities, but it's a lot harder to do than you might think.

Management Styles

Here's some more about management styles and methods. **These pages are for AQA and OCR.**

Management by Objectives sets Targets for Everyone

1) This method of management tries to **improve performance** by analysing the overall long-term **aims** or **mission** of a business and breaking them down into more specific medium-term **objectives** and **targets**.

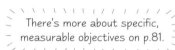
There's more about aims, missions and objectives on p.80-81.

2) Management by objectives tries to set targets for each **sector**, each **department** and each **individual employee**.

3) Management by objectives can be done by **managers choosing targets** and **telling** employees how to achieve them — this goes along with McGregor's **Theory X** of workers, and the **autocratic** style of management.

4) Management by objectives can also be done by **managers negotiating targets** with employees and agreeing how to go about meeting them — this coincides with McGregor's **Theory Y** and the **democratic** style of management.

5) Management by objectives is more likely to **succeed** when managers use a democratic style and **agree** objectives with staff.

There's more about specific, measurable objectives on p.81.

Rules for good targets:

1) Targets have to be **realistic** and **measurable**. They need to be achieved over an **agreed period of time**.

2) Managers have to **inform** everyone of the exact targets and the procedures for meeting them.

3) Managers need to organise the tasks needed to meet a target and **integrate** them with related aspects of the business.

4) Managers need to pick the **appropriate individuals** or **teams** to carry out a task or meet a target.

5) The resources needed to meet a target should be in place.

6) Management needs a method to **monitor** the **progress** of tasks and give **feedback** to everyone involved.

7) **Everyone** needs to be aware of the system of measuring **success** or **failure**.

Management by Objectives can Benefit Staff and the Whole Business

1) **Setting good objectives** forces an organisation to take a **good hard look** at itself.

2) An organisation needs to take an interest in staff as **individuals** so they can set personal employee targets.

3) Setting targets and agreeing a process to meet them can **motivate** workers.

4) **Working hard** to meet targets can help workers **improve** on their weaknesses and **develop** their skills.

5) Of course, **achieving** targets makes the business more **successful**.

There can be Problems with Management by Objectives

1) It tends to be costly in terms of **management time**.

2) Assessing the success or failure to achieve a target can be **difficult**.

3) **Personal appraisals** are particularly tricky — often the efforts of an **individual** worker are affected by the cooperation of **team-mates**.

4) It can be very difficult for management to **integrate** a range of tasks and targets within and between departments.

5) Workers who successfully meet their targets often want **promotion**, but the organisation might not actually be **able** to promote them.

6) Some workers may feel **under pressure** in trying to reach agreed targets, and may feel **threatened** by a monitoring and appraisal process.

7) Objectives go out of date quickly, so keeping them fixed in a changing business environment tends to be a bad idea. However, setting and agreeing targets for everyone can be very **time-consuming** when the firm's objectives and strategy **keep changing**.

The Captain really hated doing staff appraisals.

Management Styles

Consultation asks employees for Input on decisions

1) **Consultation** is when a manager asks employees for their **advice** and **opinions** before taking a final decision.

2) The process of consultation can be done **formally** through a **meeting** or a series of meetings. It can also be an **informal** process of having a **quick chat** with individual employees when an opportunity arises.

3) After the consultation process, it's still the **manager** who makes the decisions — and they can **ignore** their employees' opinions if they feel like it. Consultation goes with a **paternalistic** leadership style.

Delegation allows Employees to Make Decisions

1) **Delegation** is where a manager gives **another employee** the authority to make **decisions**.

2) In **large organisations** there are a **huge** number of decisions to be made — too many for senior managers to make on their own.

3) Senior managers **delegate** authority down the hierarchy to **junior managers** and **employees** so that the responsibility for making decisions is **shared out**.

4) Managers have to **trust** workers before they can delegate authority to them.

5) Employees are **motivated** by feeling that management trusts them enough to let them make real decisions.

6) Good delegation is an important feature of the **democratic** style of leadership — it **empowers** employees to make decisions without asking management. This increased responsibility helps with **employee development**.

7) Empowerment is important for **kaizen** and **quality circles**. Kaizen is Japanese for **continuous improvement** — **kaizen groups** of employees meet regularly to discuss problems and solutions, and are able to make small **improvements** in production all the time. Quality circles are **teams** who are empowered to make changes which improve quality. (See p.79 for more on this.)

Rules for healthy, happy, successful delegation

1) Managers should delegate to employees with the right **skills**, **experience** and **training**.

2) The **tasks** being delegated should be **clearly defined**, so that the employee knows **exactly** what they've got **responsibility** for. Managers should **explain** the task to the person they're delegating to.

3) The employee needs enough **resources** and **support** to make the right decisions.

4) Everyone who **needs to know** should be told who has responsibility for the task.

5) The task delegated should have some **significance** — it shouldn't be a minor, irritating chore.

6) Once they've delegated a task, the manager should keep their mitts off and **not interfere**.

The difference between consultation and delegation:

Consultation asks for opinions before making a decision. The manager **still makes the decision**, and they don't even have to take employee opinions into account.

Delegation gives the **whole responsibility** for decision-making to another employee.

Practice Questions

Q1 List three features of "good targets".
Q2 Identify three possible problems with management by objectives.
Q3 How can delegation be motivating?

Exam Questions

Q1 Explain, with examples, the essential differences between "consultation" and "delegation". (10 marks)

Q2 Outline the process which may be employed to convert the broad aims of an organisation into a series of targets. (20 marks)

I feel like delegating responsibility for this tip...

Delegation is a weight off senior management's shoulders. It's a good idea to be able to link management styles (and quality control / lean production) with methods of delegation, consultation and management by objectives. By the way — in the exam, the more reasons you can give for why things like management by objectives or delegation work, the better.

Communication in Business

Communication is all about sending and receiving information.
***These two pages are only for Edexcel.** If you're doing AQA or OCR, glide on by. Just gliiiiide right on by.*

Good Communication *is Important for business*

Good communication helps businesses to **function** efficiently. It makes it easier to **recognise** and deal with **potential problems**. Keeping workers well-informed of what's going on in the organisation increases **motivation**.

1) **Verbal** or **oral** communication means **talking**, which includes conversations between individuals, group discussions and meetings.

2) **Non-verbal communication** includes **written** communication such as letters, notices, memos, newspapers, reports, forms, etc.

3) Communication using **new technology** includes text messaging, fax, email, Internet, video conferencing, multimedia presentations, and corporate intranet.

There are *Several Categories of Business Communication*

Internal communication	Communication **within** an organisation.
External communication	Communication **between businesses**.

All these categories are in pairs of opposites.

Formal communication	**Official** communication with standard formats and **formal language**, e.g. letters, reports.
Informal communication	**Casual** communication **between employees** to pass on news and gossip — usually through **chat** and email.

Vertical communication	Information passing **upwards** or **downwards** in the **hierarchy**, e.g. manager instructs supervisor and supervisor tells workers, or salesman gives sales data to boss.
Lateral communication	Communication between people at the **same level** in the hierarchy, e.g. two nurses exchanging information about patients.

Open communication	Information available for **all employees** and the **public** as well, e.g. names and responsibilities of staff, opening hours, location of branches.
Restricted communication	Not available to everyone. May contain **personal** or **confidential** information — e.g. an employee reference or a financial statement.

Communication Technology *has Improved business communication*

1) The Internet allows businesses to **gather information** quickly. Businesses can use the Internet to **advertise** products and services to customers. They can **buy** and **sell** online — online trading is called **e-commerce**.

2) Email is electronic mail — messages sent and received via a computer network. Businesses use email for internal and external communication. It's **quick** and **efficient** — you can check your email any time. **Not everyone** has email, so businesses need other forms of communication. Many businesses also complain that employees have to spend too much **time** sorting through **unnecessary** and **junk emails**.

3) The **intranet** is the **internal computer network** within a business. Businesses can have a private **internal website** on their intranet to inform employees of corporate objectives, mission statements, etc.

4) **Video conferencing** allows people in different locations to see and hear each other via cameras and a telephone linkup. Video conferencing can be **cheaper** than paying for travel and accommodation to go to a meeting in another country. However, you miss out on the **personal contact** of face-to-face meetings.

5) **Mobile phones** and **text messaging** provide quick and efficient methods of communication. However, if your mobile isn't getting any signal reception, hard cheese.

6) **Faxes** scan printed or handwritten documents and send the information down the **phone line**. Faxing is cheap and very fast. The sender **retains** the **original document**, which can be useful.

7) **MIS** stands for **Management Information System** — this is software that enables a business to gather up-to-date information on, for example, stock, production, sales and cash flow. A good MIS can provide managers with an overview of their firm's current situation, allowing faster communication and decision-making.

Communication in Business

Different Methods of communication are suited for Different Tasks

More and more communication methods are **available** to businesses these days. It's obviously important to choose the **most appropriate method**. Factors that businesses have to consider include:

1) How **quickly** the communication needs to be delivered — fax, email and phone are very **fast**.
2) How much the business can afford to **spend** on communication. For example, it's very expensive to buy the hardware needed for video conferencing, but email and memos are very cheap.
3) Whether the communication should be **formal** or **informal** — letters are often used for formal communication, emails are often informal.
4) Whether the information is **personal** or **confidential** — some methods of communication don't guarantee confidentiality, e.g. email and fax.
5) **How many people** the communication needs to be delivered to — a meeting or presentation would be good for telling the same information to a big group of people.
6) Whether more than one form of communication is necessary. A **combination** of different methods might spread the information more effectively — e.g. a letter **and** a notice on a noticeboard.

There are a lot of Possible Barriers to communication

1) The message may contain **too much** information so it's hard to pick out the important bits — this is called **information overload**. On the other hand, the message may contain too little information to be useful.
2) The receiver may find it hard to **make out** the message — **handwriting** might be illegible, someone might **speak too quickly**, or they might speak in an **accent** which the receiver finds hard to understand.
3) The receiver might not be able to **understand** what the information actually **means** — for example, **technical** language, acronyms and abbreviations can be confusing to the receiver. Or the sender might not be very good at **explaining** things fully and clearly.
4) If there are **too many** people in the chain of communication, the original message can become **distorted**. The larger the organisation, the greater the chance that the message will get mangled between sender and receiver.
5) Not choosing the most **appropriate** method makes it harder for a message to get through — e.g. sending an urgent piece of information by letter rather than by phone or fax.
6) Sending the information to the **wrong person** in a department causes **delays**.
7) Electronic communication is prone to **glitches** — computers crash, mobile phones may not pick up a signal.
8) Communication between workers in different countries can be difficult because of **different time zones**.

> It's important to consider **potential barriers** to communication **before** sending a message — that way, you can try to **avoid** them.

Practice Questions

Q1 Name and describe four different ways of categorising business communication.
Q2 Describe five factors that might affect which form of communication is chosen. Provide examples to illustrate your choices.
Q3 When might written communication be more effective than face-to-face conversation?

Exam Questions

Q1 A relatively recent development in business has been the increasing use of electronic means of communication. Describe a possible advantage and disadvantage of both (a) emails and (b) video conferencing. (10 marks)

Q2 Outline and explain the factors which would be taken into consideration when deciding which methods of communication should be used by a business. (15 marks)

Can you hear me — I SAID can you hear me... hello... is there anyone there..?

Communication is very important in business. It isn't just about blokes with Daffy Duck socks giving management training seminars on How To Be A Really Dead Good Communicator, Like. Think about it — every objective and target and progress report has to be communicated from one person or department to another. There's a lot of communication going on.

Motivation

Motivation is what makes you work. Motivation is important in business — it's obvious that motivated employees will get more done than non-motivated employees. **These pages are for AQA, OCR and Edexcel.**

There are **Different Schools** of **Thought** about **Motivation**

Over the past 150 years industrial psychologists and sociologists have tried to figure out **what motivates workers**...

1) **Taylor** and **Scientific Management** — *people are in it for the* **Money**

1) Taylor thought that workers were motivated by **money**. He advocated a "fair day's pay for a fair day's work". However he believed workers would do the **minimum** amount of work if left to their own devices.

2) Taylor did **time and motion studies**, timing work activities with a **stopwatch**. He was in favour of **division of labour** — breaking work down into a lot of **small repetitive tasks**.

3) Taylor said managers should use time and motion studies to figure out the **most efficient** way to do a job, and then make sure every single worker did it that way. This approach is called **scientific management**.

4) Taylor also believed in paying workers according to the **quantity** they produced — and weighting pay rates so that the most **productive** workers got a **better rate**. He believed that these financial incentives would **motivate** workers and raise **productivity**.

5) Scientific management didn't go down well with workers. Increased productivity meant that **fewer workers** were needed — workers worried about losing their jobs. Taylor's approach also ignored the **demotivating** effect of doing very repetitive boring work.

6) However, **scientific management** made it possible for firms to **know** how efficiently employees were doing their jobs, and allowed them to make changes that were **sure** to **increase production**.

2) **Mayo** and **Human Relations** — *people are motivated by* **Social Factors**

1) Elton Mayo found that people achieved more when they got **positive attention**. Mayo was doing an experiment on productivity when he found that **all** workers taking part in the experiment became more productive, even the ones in the **control group**. He worked out that this was because they liked the **social attention** that they got from the experiments, and they liked working in a **group**.

2) Mayo thought management should **pay attention** to workers as individuals, and **involve** them in decision-making. He thought that firms should try to make business goals compatible with workers' goals.

3) He also thought that workers should **socialise** together — outside of work as well as at work. And that's why we have company outings to Alton Towers. So hurrah for that, I say.

3) **Maslow's Hierarchy Of Needs** — *people need* **Basics** *first*

Maslow said that people start by meeting the needs at the **bottom** of the pyramid. Once they've sorted out those needs, they can move on to the needs on the **next level** up.

Self-actualisation — meeting potential — Businesses meet these needs by giving the opportunity to develop new skills and take responsibility.

Self esteem — achievement — Businesses give employees responsibility and offer promotion.

Social Needs — friendship, teamwork — Teamworking and social outings are designed to meet these.

Safety — safe work environment with job security — Health and safety policy and secure employment contracts meet these needs.

Basic Physical Needs — food, water, shelter, clothes — Businesses meet these needs by paying workers enough and providing a warm, dry work environment.

The pyramid **looks good** — but it isn't always **obvious** which level an individual is at.

4) **Herzberg's Hygiene** and **Motivating** factors — *sort out a* **Good Environment** *first*

In the 1960s, Frederick Herzberg interviewed accountants and engineers to find out what motivated and satisfied them at work. He identified two groups of factors which influenced the motivation of workers:

1) **Hygiene factors** are things like **company policy**, **supervision**, good **working conditions**, **pay**, and good **relations** with fellow employees. They don't motivate as such, but if they **aren't good**, workers get **dissatisfied**.

2) **Motivating factors** are things like **interesting work**, personal **achievement**, **recognition** of achievement, scope for more **responsibility** and personal **development**. These factors **do** positively motivate workers.

Motivation

Financial Incentives are used to Reward and Motivate

Most working people in the UK get paid a monthly **salary** or a weekly **wage**.
There are other kinds of financial motivation, like commission and fringe benefits.

1) Workers who are paid a **weekly wage** get a set rate of so many **pounds per hour**. The more hours they work the more they get paid. There's a minimum wage — in 2004 this was £4.50 per hour. Workers usually work a **fixed working week** of about 40 hours, and get paid more for each hour of **overtime** they work.

2) Workers who get paid a monthly **salary** get so many **thousand pounds a year**, divided into 12 monthly payments. The salary isn't directly related to the number of hours worked — salaried employees work a minimum number of hours a week, and then as many hours as it takes to get the job done.

3) Some **production workers** are paid by **piece rate** — they get paid so many pounds or pence **per finished item**. The more the worker produces, the more they get paid.

4) Salespeople are usually paid **commission** — a **percentage** of the **sales** they achieve. Most sales staff get a low **basic salary** and earn commission on top of that, but some get commission only.

5) **Performance-related pay** gives more money to employees who meet their targets. Performance-related pay is linked in with employee **appraisals**. Some employees worry that they won't get a performance-related pay rise if they don't get on particularly well with the manager doing the appraisal interviews.

6) In addition to weekly/monthly pay, employees may also get **fringe benefits**. These include a **staff discount** for company products (very common in retail, not so common in aircraft manufacturing ...), employer contributions to employee **pensions**, private **medical insurance**, a company **car**, **profit-sharing** schemes and **shares** in the company.

Non-Financial Motivation — Jobs are Designed to be more Satisfying

Job design tries to **motivate** workers by **varying job tasks** and giving employees some **control** over their work.
Job design tries to give the job as many of **Herzberg's motivating factors** as possible.

1) **Job rotation** moves workers from area to area within a business to stop them getting bored.
2) **Job enlargement** gives the employee more work at the same level. It's also called **horizontal loading**.
3) **Job enrichment** gives workers more **challenging** work, and the **training** they need to do it. It gives employees more responsibility for organising their work and solving problems. It's also called **vertical loading**.
4) **Teamworking** puts workers into small teams and lets them organise their own work.
5) **Empowerment** gives employees more **control** over their working day, and a greater role in **decision-making**.
6) **Employee participation** means allowing employees to **participate** in making decisions and setting policy, giving employees **information** about what's happening in the business.
7) **Quality circles** allow small groups of workers to suggest **improvements** to productivity and quality.
8) **Multiskilling** aims to broaden the **skills** and **responsibilities** of workers.

Practice Questions

Q1 Give a brief description of Taylor's views on motivation.
Q2 Put the following needs in ascending order according to Maslow's hierarchy: friendship, job security, achievement.
Q3 Briefly explain the term "fringe benefits".
Q4 List and explain three non-financial motivators.

Exam Questions

Q1 Herzberg identified two groups of factors which influence workers' motivation.
Name these two groups, and use examples to explain how each is thought to affect motivation. (10 marks)

Q2 Colin is a checkout clerk in a supermarket, Jane is a travelling sales representative and Mike is a bricklayer. For each person, say whether they are likely to be paid according to piece rate, hourly rate or commission, and explain why. (15 marks)

But how do you motivate yourself to revise?

You need to know all the theories about motivation on the opposite page. If you happen to know any others, well, the more the merrier. It's interesting how thoughts about motivation progressed from "they're all lazy blighters" to "you need a great work environment first, then you can start with the personal development and the employee of the month award".

Size and Efficiency

When it comes to efficiency, productivity and costs per unit, bigger is better — or so it seems.
These two pages are for AQA, OCR and Edexcel.

Operations Management is about Efficiency, Productivity and Quality

1) Operations management is about managing a business to produce **quality** goods / services with **low costs** per unit, at the **right time** to meet customer needs. Managers decide on the right production methods, the right scale of production and the right amount of stock to keep.

2) Good production **efficiency** means low costs per unit. There's a **balance** between **low costs** and **quality**.

3) **Productivity** measures **output** (number of items made) in terms of **input** (number of machines used, length of time a worker takes to make an item). It can be measured as **labour productivity**, e.g. **output per worker per day** or as **capital productivity**, e.g. output per machine per week. It's related to the motivation stuff on p.66-67.

Economies of Scale mean bigger is Cheaper

Economies of scale mean that as firms **increase output**, the **costs** of producing **each item** goes down. Economies of scale are all about **unit costs**. $\implies$ $\text{Unit cost} = \dfrac{\text{Total cost}}{\text{Output}}$

Internal economies of scale increase efficiency **within** an individual firm.
There are three main internal economies of scale — **technical**, **specialisation** and **purchasing**.
There are also **financial**, **marketing** and **risk-bearing** economies of scale.

1) **Technical** economies of scale concern **production**. Large volume output uses more **efficient** production methods. Large businesses can afford to buy better, more advanced **machinery**. A large business could replace several human workers with **industrial robots**, which would increase production efficiency and reduce the cost of wages.

   "**Increased Dimensions**" is one kind of technical economy of scale. For example, a **large office** has more desks and workers than a small office, but it only needs **one reception desk** and **one handyman** — the **same** as a **small** office. It also applies to **equipment** — you don't need a lot more steel to make a 1000-litre barrel than you do to make a 500-litre barrel (it's true, you don't need twice the steel).

2) **Specialisation** economies of scale are to do with **employees**. Large businesses can employ managers with **specialist skills** and separate them out into specialised departments — instead of paying **external specialists** to do the work, or having one **jack-of-all-trades** manager doing lots of different jobs. For example, a large business might have its own market researchers, and its own accountants and lawyers. Having in-house specialists is **cheaper** than paying external firms to do the work.

3) **Purchasing** economies of scale are to do with **discounts**. Large businesses can negotiate **discounts** when **buying supplies**. They can get bigger discounts and longer credit periods than their smaller competitors.

4) **Financial** economies of scale are to do with **borrowing money**. Large firms borrow at **lower rates of interest** than smaller firms. Lenders feel more comfortable lending money to a big firm than a small firm.

5) **Marketing** economies of scale are related to **promotion costs**. The cost of an ad campaign is a **fixed cost**. A business with a large output can share out the cost over more products than a business with a low output.

6) **Risk-bearing** economies of scale are to do with **diversification**. Large businesses have a greater ability to bear **risk** than their small competitors. They don't need to put all their eggs in one basket, or all their money on one horse. They're big enough to **diversify** into several different **markets** or cater to several different **market segments**.

External Economies of Scale make a Whole Industry or Area more efficient

External economies of scale happen when industries are concentrated in small geographical areas.

1) Having an **established network of suppliers** gives economies of scale. Locating close together means firms can easily play local suppliers off against each other, which increases quality and reduces price.

2) A good skilled **labour supply** makes an industry more efficient. This is most important in industries where training is **expensive** or takes a long time. For example, software developers in "Silicon Valley" know that plenty of programmers who are qualified to fill their vacancies **already** live within driving distance.

3) Local firms benefit from good **infrastructure** — like an airport, a motorway or good rail links. For example, Dublin's tourist industry had a massive boost in profits after Ryanair started **cheap flights** to Dublin.

Size and Efficiency

Diseconomies of Scale — being bigger can be Bad News, too

Diseconomies of scale are things that make unit costs of production rise as output rises.
They happen because large firms are harder to manage than small firms.

Diseconomies of scale come from bad **motivation**, bad **communication** and bad **coordination**.

1) In a big firm, it's hard to **coordinate** activities between different departments. It's important to keep all the different departments working towards the **same objectives** and pushing in the **same direction**. In a large business, it's hard to make sure that managers aren't setting objectives that **don't go together** with the objectives of the rest of the business. Poor coordination makes a business **drift off course**.

2) **Communication** between people and departments is harder in a big business. It can be **slow** and **difficult** to get messages to the right people, especially when there are **long chains of command**. The **amount** of information circulating in a business can increase at a faster rate than the business is actually growing.

3) It can be harder to **motivate** people in a large business. In a **small** business, managers are in **regular contact** with staff, and it's easier for everyone to feel like they **belong** and that they're working towards the same aims. When people feel like they **don't really belong**, and that there's **no real point** to what they're doing, they get **demotivated**. Poor motivation leads to reduced productivity, increased labour turnover and **absenteeism** (employees skiving off and calling in sick).

Diseconomies of scale are caused by problems with management. Strong leadership, delegation and decentralisation can all help keep diseconomies of scale at bay, and keep costs down.

1) It's much **easier** to measure and quantify **economies** of scale than **diseconomies** of scale.

2) For example, it's **easy** to calculate the **cost** of a new piece of machinery and work out its **cost per unit** for different levels of output.

3) But, it's **hard** to work out exactly how **motivated** employees will be at different levels of output, or how bad **communication problems** will be at various output levels.

Diseconomies of scale are mainly qualitative rather than quantitative.

Businesses have to Choose the Right Scale of production

A business needs to get **output** to levels where **economies of scale** make **unit costs** as **low** as possible — without letting it get to the point where **diseconomies of scale** start pushing unit costs up again.

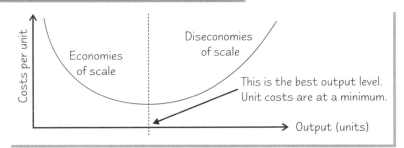

Practice Questions

Q1 Identify three benefits that firms would hope to get by increasing their size.

Q2 Explain the difference between internal and external economies of scale.

Q3 Give an example of a diseconomy of scale.

Q4 Which are easiest to measure, economies of scale or diseconomies of scale? Explain your answer.

Exam Questions

Q1 Discuss the economies of scale that will be of most benefit to a large manufacturing firm such as Dyson. (4 marks)

Q2 To what extent should a business accept diseconomies of scale as inevitable? (6 marks)

So it isn't what you do with it, it's how big it is that counts...

If you remember anything from these pages, remember "bigger is cheaper, but too big and you've got problems". If you want to get the marks for analysis and evaluation, you'd be well advised to learn the various ways that economies of scale can happen. That way you can mould the idea of economy of scale to the particular situation given in an exam question.

Capacity Utilisation

It's inefficient to not use machinery or premises which you've paid for. It's not cost effective to produce too much stock and have it lying around in warehouses. **This page is for AQA, OCR and Edexcel.**

Capacity is Maximum Output with the Resources Currently Available

1) The **capacity** of an organisation is the **maximum** output that it can produce in a given period without buying any more fixed assets — machinery, factory space, etc.

2) Capacity depends on the **number of employees** and how skilled they are.

3) Capacity depends on the **technology** the business has — what **machinery** they have, what state it's in, what kind of computer system they have, etc.

4) Capacity depends on the kind of production **process** the business uses.

5) The amount of **investment** in the business is also a factor.

Capacity Utilisation is How Much Capacity is being Used

$$\text{Capacity Utilisation} = \frac{\text{Output}}{\text{Capacity}} \times 100 \ \%$$

For example: a hotel with half its rooms booked out has a capacity utilisation of 50%. A clothing factory with output of 70 000 shirts per month and a maximum capacity of 100 000 shirts is running at 70% capacity utilisation. Capacity utilisation depends on **demand**.

Check out the capacity on that...

Under-utilisation is Inefficient and pushes Costs Up

1) Low capacity utilisation is called **under-utilisation**.

2) It's **inefficient** because the business isn't getting use out of machines and facilities it's **already paid for**.

3) The **fixed cost** of the firm's assets is spread over **less output** — which means that **unit costs go up**. This reduces profit margins, and makes the product **less profitable**.

90% Capacity Utilisation can be better than 100% capacity utilisation

High capacity utilisation is better than low capacity utilisation. However, 100% capacity utilisation has drawbacks.

1) The business may have to turn away potential **customers**.

2) There's no **downtime** — machines are on **all the time**. If a machine has a problem, it'll cause delays and bottlenecks as work piles up waiting for the problem to be fixed. There's no time for equipment maintenance, which can reduce the life of machinery.

3) There's no **margin of error**. Everything has to be perfect first time, which causes **stress** to managers. **Mistakes** are more likely when everyone's working flat out.

4) The business can't **temporarily increase output** for seasonal demand or one-off orders.

5) If output is greater than demand, there'll be **surplus stock** hanging about waiting to be sold. It's not good to have valuable **working capital** tied up in stock.

> Businesses should plan production levels to achieve **almost** full capacity utilisation.

Businesses Change capacity utilisation to match Predicted Demand

1) Demand **changes** over time, so firms must think about demand in the **future** as well as the current demand.

2) The key to **long-term** success is planning **capacity** changes to match long-term changes in demand. Market research helps predict future demand, but it's not 100% certain. There's always an element of risk.

3) **Short-term** changes in **capacity utilisation** provide **flexibility**. Firms should **temporarily** increase capacity utilisation if an increase in demand isn't expected to continue in the **long term** — for example, with seasonal products like Christmas crackers, products heading towards decline in their life cycle, and one-off special orders.

4) **Long-term** solutions end up giving **lower unit costs** — as long as **predictions** of demand turn out to be **true**.

Capacity Utilisation

Capacity utilisation can be **Increased** by **Increasing Production** and **Demand**

1) Businesses can use **more capacity** by using their facilities for **more** of the **working week**. They can have staff working in two or three **shifts** in a day, and they can have people working on weekends and bank holidays.

2) Businesses can **increase** their **staff levels** in the long run by recruiting new permanent staff. In the short run they can employ **temporary staff** or get their staff to work **overtime**.

3) Businesses also increase their capacity utilisation by increasing **productivity**. They can re-organise production by reallocating staff to the busiest areas, and they can increase employee **motivation**.

4) **Subcontracting** is when a business uses its **facilities** to do work on behalf of **another business**. For example, a manufacturer of washing powder might make washing powder for a **supermarket** and package it with the supermarket's own label. It's better to use facilities to make goods for a **competitor** and make a little money than it is to leave **expensive machinery** sitting around doing **nothing**.

There's **no point** in producing more than you can **sell**.
Businesses need to **stimulate demand** as well as increasing production.

1) Businesses stimulate demand by changing the **marketing mix**. They can change the **promotion** of a product, change its **price** or its **distribution** (see p.20-25 for more on the marketing mix).

2) **Subcontracting** is a way of increasing demand. When you allow your machines to be used to make products for a competitor, you know that you'll be able to sell those products to the competitor — you're not just relying on demand for your own brand of product.

Capacity utilisation can be **Increased** by **Reducing Capacity**

1) If a business is **operating under capacity** and they think that demand isn't going to go up in the future, they need to **reduce their capacity** by shutting part of their production facilities. This is called **rationalising** or **downsizing**. It's become popular with large firms who want to stay competitive by cutting their production costs.

2) Businesses can reduce capacity in the **short term** by stopping **overtime** or reducing the length of the working week, allocating staff to **other work** in the business, and by not renewing **temporary contracts**.

3) Businesses can reduce capacity in the **long term** by not **replacing** staff as they retire (natural wastage), making staff **redundant**, and by **selling off** factories or equipment.

4) An area of work with low capacity utilisation can be **subcontracted out** to a specialist firm. The staff who had been doing the work can either be made **redundant** or moved to more **productive** work inside the business.

OCR and AQA

Practice Questions

Q1 Write down the formula for capacity utilisation.
Q2 Why is under-utilisation a bad thing?
Q3 What is "subcontracting"?
Q4 Businesses can increase capacity utilisation by producing more. How else can they increase capacity utilisation?

Exam Questions

Q1 Discuss why 95% capacity utilisation is considered better for a firm than 100%. (4 marks)

Q2 Analyse how a manufacturer of fashion clothing should expand their business if recent growth has led to capacity utilisation reaching 100%. (10 marks)

She cannae take any more, Jim...

Capacity utilisation crops up elsewhere. Under-utilisation is a consequence of low demand. When a business launches a product, capacity utilisation starts out low and then builds up as demand for the new product increases. It's very much worth your while to know how businesses take action to get their capacity utilisation to round about 90% or so.

Types of Production

There are several ways of organising production. The key difference is between lovingly hand crafting every item, or cranking identical products out of a machine. **This page is for AQA, OCR and Edexcel.**

Job Production *is* One-off *production*

1) Job production produces unique products or services. Each item is finished before the next item is started.

2) Job production is **labour intensive**, using skilled workers. It has a high **labour to capital ratio** — i.e. it uses a lot of labour and doesn't need much capital investment.

3) It produces **small quantities**, often **made to order**. Products can be **tailored** to customer requirements.

4) Examples include hairdressers, wedding dress designers, hand-made cards or jewellery and original paintings.

Advantages of Job Production	Disadvantages of Job Production
High **quality** products, specific to customer requirements.	Skilled labour is **expensive**.
High **added value**, so even low sales can make a profit.	Low output means **no economies of scale**.
Good **customer service** helps the business get repeat sales.	It takes **time** to make products to order — there are **no impulse purchases**. Customers go elsewhere for instant service.
Set-up costs are **low** — big machines aren't used.	There's **low capacity utilisation** of **equipment** — skilled workers use a variety of tools rather than one tool all the time.

Flow Production *is* Mass *production on an* Assembly Line

1) Flow production is a **continuous** process where products are assembled in a series of stages.

2) This production method makes a large volume of identical, **standardised** products.

3) Flow production often uses a **production line** where components pass along a **conveyor belt**. At each stage of the process a worker does a **set task** as the components pass by. They do the same task all day so they don't have to be skilled. Car assembly lines are a good example.

4) Flow production has **high set-up costs** — production line machines are **expensive**. Flow production is **capital intensive**, and has a **low** labour to capital ratio.

5) Flow production needs **high-volume sales** to reach **break even** point — because the **fixed costs** of machinery are so high. It isn't suitable for low demand, or for demand that goes up and down a lot.

Advantages of Flow Production	Disadvantages of Flow Production
Low unit costs due to economies of scale.	High **start-up costs**.
Production is **fast** and **efficient**.	Needs **constant, predictable demand**.
Low levels of **work in progress**, so doesn't need much storage space.	Flow production needs careful **planning** to avoid hold-ups. The whole process has to keep moving all the time.

Batch Production *makes* Identical Batches *of product*

1) Products pass through each stage of the production process in **batches**.

2) All items in a batch are **identical** although changes can be made from batch to batch. It's like a **compromise** between **job** and **flow** production.

3) A set of batches of **different components** can be made on the **same machine** using batch production and then put together in a separate operation. For example, one machine makes a batch of 5000 widgets in week 1 and a batch of 5000 wossnames in week 2. Then in week 3 the widgets and wossnames get assembled together.

Advantages of Batch Production	Disadvantages of Batch Production
Lower unit costs than with **job** production.	**Higher** unit costs than with **flow** production.
Output is **higher** than with job production.	It takes **time** to **retool** machines to make the next batch.
Batch production is **flexible**.	Batch production needs careful **planning** and **coordination**.
Lots of **different components** can be made with **one machine**, which helps save costs.	There are **high** levels of **work in progress**. One batch can sit around until another batch is finished before assembly.

Types of Production

Deciding **Which Method** to use depends on **Several Factors**

1) **Customer requirements**. Firms in a market where customers demand unique and tailor-made products will use job production. Markets where customers demand low prices and accept standardised products will use flow production.

2) **Demand**. Flow production is only possible with **high** and **unchanging demand**. Batch production may be more suitable if customers want a degree of choice.

3) **Resources**. Firms with a pool of highly skilled labour will naturally be good at job production and are likely to experience poor motivation if they try to move away from this. A business without enough sources of finance wouldn't be able to introduce flow production even if they wanted to.

4) The **aims and objectives** of the business. An objective of **maximising productivity** and **profit** goes with **flow** production. An objective of building a **personal relationship** with a customer goes with **job production**.

There are **Balances** — **Labour** vs **Capital** and **Flexibility** vs **Productivity**

Labour vs Capital

1) Job production is **labour intensive**, but doesn't need much **capital**. It has a high labour to capital ratio, in other words.

2) Flow production is **capital intensive**, but doesn't require much **skilled labour**. It has a low labour to capital ratio.

3) Technological advances make it possible for flow production to use **industrial robots** instead of human workers. Industrial robots are very **expensive**, which makes the **labour to capital ratio** even **lower** than for traditional assembly line production.

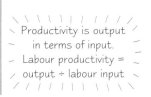
Productivity is output in terms of input.
Labour productivity = output ÷ labour input

Flexibility vs Productivity

1) Job production is **very flexible**, but it only produces small amounts of product per worker.

2) Flow production is **inflexible**, but produces huge amounts of product per worker.

3) Batch production is fairly **flexible**.

Production methods affect **Competitiveness Abroad**

1) Production facilities in the UK are different to production facilities in the developing world. UK factories are more **technologically developed**. There are fewer workers, but more expensive machinery.

2) The **developing world** has a ready source of cheap skilled and unskilled labour. Job production is cheaper in the developing world. It can also be cheap to have a factory using flow or batch production in the developing world, as long as the factory is reasonably low-tech, with a relatively high labour/capital ratio.

3) For **developed world** businesses to keep up their international **competitiveness**, they should compete in the **high-tech** areas where they have the edge.

Practice Questions

Q1 Describe the main differences between job, batch and flow production in terms of set-up costs, unit costs, product variety and output.

Q2 State four factors to consider when choosing a method of production.

Q3 Why might a business using production methods with a high labour/capital ratio lose out to foreign competition?

Exam Questions

Q1 Why might the exclusive sports car manufacturer TVR use job production when Ford uses flow production? (10 marks)

Q2 Why might flow production increase productivity in the short term then reduce it in the longer term? (8 marks)

I'm not going to make the obvious gag about bakers...

As far as basic facts go, you sort this lot out into three main headings — job production, flow production and batch production. You have to know the facts about what they are, how much they cost to set up, how efficient they are, etc. You also need to be able to evaluate which method might be suitable for a given business.

Types of Production

Lean production is all about stamping out wasteful habits and turning the business into one lean, mean, making-things machine. It's actually worth having a gander at the pages on stock (p.76-77) as well, cos it's all part of a glorious interconnected web of operational efficiency. **These pages are for all three boards — AQA, Edexcel and OCR.**

Lean Production aims to Reduce Costs by Cutting Out Waste

1) **Lean production** is a modern business philosophy based on the idea of increasing **efficiency** by cutting out all forms of **waste**, and really **streamlining** production.

2) Lean production tries to use less **time**, **space**, **raw materials** and **money**. Lean production is **more productive** than traditional mass production — it uses **less input** to get the **same output**.

3) Lean production techniques include **just-in-time** production (JIT), **cell** production, **continuous improvement** (Kaizen — see p.79) and **time-based management**.

4) **Training employees** for lean production costs money. Businesses need to take care that these costs don't outweigh the cost savings that they get from lean production.

Just-In-Time (JIT) reduces Costs but needs Very Effective Management

1) **Just-in-time** (**JIT**) production aims to have as little **stock** as possible — ideally, raw materials come in one door, are made into products and go straight out another door — all **just in time** for delivery to customers.

2) JIT is based on very efficient **stock control**. **Kanban** is the name given to the system used to **trigger repeat orders**. When employees reach coloured kanban cards towards the end of a batch of components, they order more. Kanban cards make sure that the **supply** of raw materials is **dictated** by the **demand** — there's no need for lots of stock.

See p.61 for more on management and teamworking.

3) More than anything else, JIT depends on **cooperation**:

- Unhappiness in the **workforce** leading to low productivity, absenteeism (sickies) or strikes will cause the system to break down. **People-centred management** can help to create a satisfying working environment. In contrast to traditional management approaches, workers are treated as valued **team members**, are involved in decision-making, and are given increased responsibility and opportunities for development.

- JIT also requires **flexible working**. Production is tied to customer **demand**, so **employees** need to be able to work on the most urgent tasks, **coordinating** their efforts in order to keep production moving. This is different from traditional repetitive factory work, and fits in nicely with people-centred management.

- Slow or unreliable deliveries from **suppliers** will make JIT production unworkable. Businesses using JIT usually have links and long-term partnerships with suppliers. For example, JIT suppliers for MG Rover have staff on site at the MG Rover factory checking stock levels and coordinating deliveries several times a day.

Benefits of just-in-time production:

1) The cost of **storage space** (e.g. **rent**) for materials, work in progress and finished goods is reduced.

2) **Cash flow** is improved — working capital isn't tied up in work in progress.

3) **Productivity** is higher — JIT uses less material, space, time and money to get the same output.

4) There's greater **flexibility** because products are built to order.

5) There's **less waste** — there's no old, damaged or out-of-date stock lying around.

Drawbacks of just-in-time production:

1) **Supplier delays** can cause production to **stop** immediately. There's no stock to keep things going.

2) **Strikes** bring **supply** to a halt. There's no **finished stock** to supply customers when workers down tools.

3) **Without** raw material stocks, a business can't respond quickly to a **sudden** increase in **demand**. Businesses with seasonal or hard-to-forecast demand don't usually use JIT systems — they'd be **too complex** to work.

4) Products have to be **perfect first time** — there isn't enough stock available to replace faulty products.

Just-In-Time vs. Just-In-Case — Lean production vs. Economies of Scale

Traditional businesses work on a **just in case** principle. They keep stocks of **raw materials**, **work in progress** and **finished items** — all just in case they're needed to meet sudden demands.

With just-in-case production, orders from suppliers are **large** and **infrequent**. The business can get discounts from ordering in bulk — just-in-time production can't have these **purchasing economies of scale**.

Just-in-case production tends to keep producing **large volumes** so it can benefit from **economies of scale** — this large-scale production, which isn't tied to **demand**, means the business can end up with huge **stockpiles** of finished items.

Types of Production

Cell Production cuts out waste and Improves Motivation

1) Cell production divides production up into **self-contained teams** (cells) of employees. Each cell is responsible for one stage of the production process.

2) Workers in the team do a **range of tasks** to get the job done. They don't get stuck with one repetitive task all day, as with traditional assembly lines. Each cell is usually arranged in a **horseshoe** shape. Products circulate around the horseshoe, and then they're passed to the cell doing the next stage of the process.

3) Cells **self-check** the quality of the work they've done (see p.78) which helps cut out **mistakes**. The next cell along in the production process can send work back if it isn't right.

4) Because cells work on **small batches** of items, there's almost **no** work in progress. Work in progress is a form of **stock** — it takes up space and uses up working capital.

5) Workers **organise themselves** to perform whatever tasks are **necessary**. This helps with motivation — people like to organise themselves. It also avoids **bottlenecks** building up behind one slow worker.

6) The **teamworking** atmosphere and **job enrichment opportunities** that you get with cell production help improve employee motivation — which leads to even more productivity improvements.

Time-based Management — going faster and faster and faster...

1) **Time-based management** tries to speed up the **time** that each process takes.

2) In **research and development** managers try to speed up testing and research tasks.

3) The **marketing** department works to speed up **market research** and product launches.

4) In **production**, computerised machinery and skilled staff combine to allow **shorter** but more **frequent** production runs. This cuts down **lead time** (the time between getting an order and completing it — see p.77). **JIT production** is a good example of this (see p.74).

5) **Simultaneous engineering** is where different aspects of product development are done at the **same time**.

6) Faster production can give **big cost savings** and **marketing benefits** — such as launching new products ahead of major competitors. That sounds worth a little effort.

The Advantages of Lean Production depend on Customers and Competitors

1) Lean producers are more **flexible** than mass producers, and tend to have **small volume** production runs. They have a bigger edge over mass manufacturers when **product life cycles** are **short**, i.e. when fashions change quickly. They benefit when customers demand more new, fashionable, "now" products — which they certainly seem to be doing these days...

2) Of course, the advantage your business gets from lean production depends on what **other businesses** are up to. If they've all got the lean production bug as well, you won't get as much of a **competitive advantage**.

Practice Questions

Q1 State three benefits and three drawbacks of just-in-time production methods.
Q2 Identify four key differences between mass and lean production.
Q3 Why might cell production improve employee motivation?
Q4 What is time-based management?

Exam Questions

Q1 What problems might a large manufacturer of skiing equipment experience when moving over to a just-in-time production system? (4 marks)

Q2 To what extent do you agree that all firms should use lean production methods? (12 marks)

Just-in-time — sometimes it just works, sometimes it just doesn't...

Lean production and just-in-time are great for cutting waste and making things efficient. They aren't always the be-all and end-all, because they don't suit all businesses. If a business has flakey suppliers who don't deliver on time, just-in-time production will be a disaster. Cell production is a good way to motivate, avoid bottlenecks and improve quality.

Stock

Good stock management is a balance between keeping stocks as low as possible, to save money, and avoiding running out of stock, causing inconvenience to customers and losing revenue. ***These pages are for AQA, OCR and Edexcel.***

Businesses need Stock — Materials, Work in Progress and Finished Items

1) **Raw materials**, **work in progress** and **finished items** are all types of **stock**.

2) **Raw materials** are all the things needed in the production of an item. Businesses **need** raw materials in stock so that machines and workers don't sit **idle** waiting for raw materials to arrive.

3) **Work in progress** (or **WIP** for short) are items part-way through the production process.

4) **Finished products** are complete items in the warehouse that haven't been **sold** yet. Finished stock is there to satisfy customer demand **instantly**.

5) Businesses need stock to **keep production going** and to cope with customer **demand**. Businesses without enough raw materials can't produce finished goods. Businesses without enough finished goods in stock can't respond to sudden customer demand.

It's Costly to hold lots of Stock

1) **Storage costs** are the most **obvious cost** of holding stock. Storage costs include rent for the warehouse and also the non-obvious costs of heating, lighting, refrigeration, security etc. Don't forget those.

2) **Wastage costs** are the costs of **throwing away** useless stock. The longer a business holds stock, the more likely it is to create waste. Stocks get **physically damaged** as time goes on, and they can also go **out of fashion**.

3) **Opportunity cost** is the cost of **investing** money in stock instead of **something else**. Capital tied up in stock is **unproductive** and could be used more productively elsewhere, such as financing a marketing campaign.

The value of stock a business is holding is recorded on the **balance sheet** (see p.47), and features in the trading part of the **profit and loss account** (as opening and closing stock — see p.48).

Buffer Stock is the Minimum amount of stock a Business Needs

A business needs a **minimum** level of stock so it **won't run out** of materials or finished goods. Running out of **raw materials** or **work in progress** means that production grinds to a **halt** — very bad news. Running out of **product** means that customers have to be **turned away** — more bad news. This minimum stock level is called **buffer stock**.

1) The level of buffer stock depends on the **warehouse space** available.

2) Buffer stock levels also depend on the **kind** of product you're storing — a **perishable** food item will have lower buffer stock levels than something which keeps, to reduce the risk of it **going off**.

3) The level of buffer stock depends on the **rate** at which the business **uses up** its stocks. If it goes through stocks like a knife through butter, it'll need to hold more stock.

4) **Suppliers** are a massive factor in working out buffer stock levels. The **lead time** is the time it takes for goods to **arrive** after ordering them from the supplier. The **longer** the lead time, the **more buffer stocks** you need to hold — if customer demand suddenly went up, you wouldn't want to wait a long time for stocks to arrive from the supplier. A **short lead time** means you can have **small** buffer stocks and top them up as and when you need to.

Stock, stock, lovely stock.
Piles and piles of beautiful stock...

Just-in-time production takes
short lead times to the extreme
(see p.74 for more on JIT).

Stock

Stock Control Charts help control Stock Management

Stock control charts allow managers to **analyse** and **control** stock over a period of time — as shown below.
Have a good look at the diagram. It'll make stock control easier to understand. Plus, if you're doing **OCR** or **Edexcel**,
you can be asked to **draw** or **analyse** a stock control chart, so best familiarise yourself with how that's done.

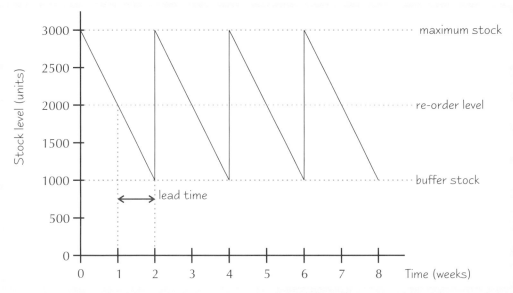

1) The **buffer stock level** is **1000 units**. The **lead time** is 1 week, and the
business goes through **1000 units** each week. That means they have to
re-order stock when they've got **2000** units left — just so they don't go below
their buffer stock level. 2000 units is the **re-order level**. (Catchy name, huh.)

2) The business re-orders **2000 units** of stock each time. This takes them back
up to their **maximum stock level** of 3000 units.

Stock Rotation has to go in the right sequence — First In, First Out

1) Stock rotation means **arranging** stock so it's **used** in the order it was **purchased**.

2) Employees re-stocking products put the **new** items at the **back** of the shelf so they're used last.
This is called "**first in, first out**" or FIFO for short.

3) If they put new stock at the front of the shelf, the stock at the back may **never** be used until it's
out of date. This isn't such bad news for rolls of cloth, but it's disastrous for pints of milk. Ew.

Practice Questions

Q1 Define the three types of stock a business might hold.

Q2 Draw and label a stock control chart.

Q3 Describe the costs associated with holding high stocks.

Q4 Why is stock rotated?

Exam Questions

Q1 Discuss the factors that determine how much stock an audio equipment factory would hold. (10 marks)

Q2 Examine the potential benefits of efficient stock control to a small manufacturing firm. (8 marks)

Do gravy manufacturers have minimum stock levels?

*It's important to have the right level of stock. Too much, and you're paying to have stock sitting around for no reason, and
tying up cash for no reason. Too little, and production will grind to a halt, or customers will stalk out of the shop in disgust
because you've run out of ice lollies on the hottest day of year. Also, you need good stock to make good soup.*

Quality Control

Increased competition means firms now compete through quality as well as price. High quality increases revenues and reduces costs so it's more important now than ever before. **These pages are for AQA, OCR and Edexcel.**

Good Quality products and services Meet Customer Needs

1) Products have to be **fit** for the **purpose** they're made for. For example, the quality of a tin opener is judged by how well it opens tins.

2) The **customer's opinion** of quality is the most important one. Businesses should use **market research** to check customers are satisfied with product quality.

Poor Quality Reduces Profits

1) In the **dark old days**, managers thought quality improvements **increased costs**, so they only went for **slight** quality improvements which wouldn't cost very much.

2) Enlightened managers think of the **opportunity cost** of **not** having a great quality product. They go for high quality as a way of actually **reducing costs** and increasing revenue.

Quality improvements reduce costs:

1) Fewer **raw materials** and less **worker** and **machinery** time get used up by **mistakes**.

2) You don't need as much **advertising** and **promotional** gubbins to persuade **shops** to stock high quality goods.

3) You don't need to spend as much on **marketing** to attract **new customers**.

4) You need fewer **customer care staff** because there aren't as many **complaints** to deal with.

5) There are fewer **refunds** and fewer claims on **warranties**.

Quality improvements increase revenue:

1) You don't need to **discount** prices to sell **damaged stock** when there isn't any damaged or "seconds" quality stock.

2) You can **charge more** — high quality products allow for **premium pricing**.

3) High quality products improve the **image** and **reputation** of the business.

4) Quality goods and services make it easy to keep **existing customers**.

5) A good reputation for quality brings in **new customers**.

Quality Control and Quality Assurance are Different Things

Quality control means **detecting** mistakes — **checking** goods for **faults** or **poor quality**.
Quality assurance means **preventing** mistakes — **designing** the production process so **faults don't happen**.

1) The traditional quality control approach assumes that errors are **unavoidable**. It says that the best you could do was to **detect errors** and **put them right** before customers bought the products.

2) Traditionally, **quality control inspectors** checked other people's work. This has drawbacks — inspectors are additional staff and need to be paid, and employees feel distrusted and demotivated.

3) With modern approaches to quality control, workers check their own work. This is called **self-checking**. **Empowering** employees to check the quality of their own work can be highly **motivating**.

4) Thinking that errors and faults are inevitable gives the production department the idea that they **needn't bother** to avoid mistakes. The quality control inspectors will always pick up mistakes later.

5) Under a quality assurance system, it's **everyone's responsibility** to produce good work. Everyone should try to get it **right first time**. Workers can **reject** components or work in progress if it isn't up to standard. They don't pass the poor quality off as **someone else's problem**. Workers are responsible for passing on good quality work in progress to the next stage of the production process.

6) **Training** is really important for quality assurance. Workers have to be trained to produce good quality products and services. New recruits get this as part of **induction**. Experienced workers need **retraining**.

Quality, motivation and training are linked.

7) Workers must be **motivated** and **committed** to quality for quality assurance schemes to work.

8) The ultimate aim of quality assurance is to create a culture of **zero defects**.

Quality Control

There are Several Approaches to Quality Assurance

Total Quality Management is the ultimate, extreme version of Quality Assurance

1) **Total Quality Management** (TQM) means the **whole workforce** has to be committed to quality improvements. The idea is to **build quality** into every department and not let quality get squeezed out.

2) With TQM, every employee has to try to **satisfy customers** — both **external** customers that the business sells things to, and **internal** customers within the business.

3) It takes **time** to introduce TQM. Employees can be **demotivated** — TQM can seem like a lot of extra work. Workers need **training** so that they see quality as their responsibility. **Rewards** for quality can be motivating.

OCR and AQA

Kaizen is Japanese for "continuous improvement"

1) The **kaizen** approach means that employees should be **improving** their work slightly **all the time**, instead of making one-off improvements when management tell them to.

2) For kaizen to work, employees at the bottom of the hierarchy have to be given control over **decision-making** so that they can actually **implement** quality improvements.

OCR and AQA — *OCR and AQA* — *OCR and AQA*

Benchmarking looks for top quality in other businesses, and learns from their example

1) Benchmarking studies **other businesses** with excellent **quality standards**, and aims to **adopt** their **methods**.

2) Benchmarking isn't always appropriate. **Competitors** are unlikely to **share** important information, and **working practices** can't always be transferred between different **corporate cultures**.

Edexcel

Quality circles are groups of employees who work on quality issues

1) Quality circles include employees from **various departments**. They meet to **identify** and **solve** problems.

2) Quality circles can be very effective at raising quality because they utilise the **knowledge** and **expertise** of factory floor staff — as long as staff are **motivated** by the initiative to share their thoughts and suggestions.

Edexcel — *Edexcel* — *Edexcel*

Quality Awards are Evidence of High Standards

1) **BS 5750** is an award given out by the **British Standards Institution** to firms with good quality assurance systems. **ISO 9000** is the **European** quality award. It's equivalent to BS 5750.

2) To get the award, a business must set **quality targets**, make sure their production process **achieves** these targets, and continually **monitor** production quality. This process can **cost money**.

3) The British Standards Institute **don't care** too much what these standards actually are, only that the business has systems in place to meet its own targets.

4) BS 5750 and ISO 9000 can be used in **marketing** to win the trust of customers.

Practice Questions

Q1 Give two reasons why high quality reduces costs.

Q2 What's the difference between quality control and quality assurance?

Q3 Explain the concept of kaizen.

Exam Questions

Q1 Examine the potential costs and benefits of obtaining ISO 9000 certification. (6 marks)

Q2 The Managing Director of Bhatia Textiles decides to introduce Total Quality Management to the business. Explain why employees may be resistant to TQM, and suggest how it might be successfully introduced. (10 marks)

AS Examiners — the ultimate quality control inspectors...

It's pretty obvious that good quality is important in business. People don't like paying for things that aren't any good. There are different ways to go about making sure that products and services are of good quality — one important difference is between quality control inspections of finished products and quality assurance systems for the whole production process.

Setting Objectives

Businesses set aims and objectives to provide long-term targets. They then develop strategies to achieve these objectives. On the way to a big target, they set lots of little targets to ensure they're on the right track. **For AQA, Edexcel and OCR.**

Corporate Planning *starts with* Corporate Aims

1) **Corporate aims** are the long-term ambitions of a business — the reason the business exists. These are quite general, e.g. "to offer our customers the best value for money possible" and businesses use them to create a common **vision (or mission)** for all employees to work towards.

2) **Values** are the beliefs and assumptions that staff have about their work. These unwritten attitudes influence how people work and make decisions. Collectively, they represent the **culture** of the company.

3) **Mission statements** are written descriptions of business aims which businesses use to **inform** stakeholders and **motivate** employees.

4) **Strategic objectives** are medium-term to long-term targets that businesses set to help them achieve corporate aims. Strategic objectives are set by **senior management**, at the top of the business hierarchy.

5) **Operational** (or **tactical**) **objectives** set targets for the day-to-day operations of the business, to make sure it meets its strategic objectives. Operational objectives are set by managers within each **department**.

6) **Individual objectives** set targets for each individual employee.

The hierarchy of objectives

Corporate aims and mission statement

↓

Strategic objectives

↓

Operational and tactical objectives

↓

Individual objectives

Examples:

Corporate aim: To be the biggest in our market.

Strategic objective: To reduce the number of competitors.

Operational objective: To get advertising in all major newspapers.

Individual objective: To negotiate good prices for quarter-page advertisements in the Times, Telegraph and Guardian.

Corporate planning is done formally in big companies. In smaller and simpler businesses, it can be a lot more casual, and objectives can be pretty much assumed.

Mission Statements *are written statements of* Corporate Aims

1) Mission statements **communicate** to all stakeholders what the company is trying to achieve. They set out what the business does, why they're doing it, what service they aim to provide to customers, and generally how they are going to go about providing the best service.

2) Mission statements can be **short** and **memorable**:

"McIvor and Wilson works to make cough medicine that makes people's coughs better."

Or they can be wildly long-winded:

"Our purpose at McIvor and Wilson is to be a leader in the over-the-counter cough mixture market. We add value for our customers and shareholders by anticipating the changing needs of our customers and responding with high-quality and innovative products. As part of our caring ethos, we seek to give back to our community through proactive partnerships and programmes."

3) Mission statements are intended to **motivate** employees and encourage **everyone** in the organisation to work towards the organisation's ultimate aim. To do this, it's best to **involve** as many levels of staff and **stakeholder** groups as possible in formulating the statement. Everyone in the business should know what the mission statement **means**, **agree** with it, and know how **they** can contribute to "make it so".

4) Mission statements need to be **reviewed** from time to time, to check that they haven't gone out of date and that they're still suitable for where the business is now and where it needs to be in the future.

5) Mission statements are often criticised because they **cost** a lot of **money** and management **time** to create. To be worthwhile, a mission statement must give benefits that **outweigh** the **costs** of writing it.

6) Sometimes mission statements are only **publicity tools**, with no real substance behind them.

Remember, the mission statement states what a company wishes to achieve — but **stating** this and **achieving** it are two different things. The **effectiveness** of a mission statement depends on **what it gets people to do**, not on the fancy words it uses.

Setting Objectives

Corporate Objectives need to be SMART

SMART stands for Specific, Measurable, Agreed, Realistic and Time specific.

Specific objectives set out exactly what the business means to do.

Measurable objectives make it easy to monitor progress, and tell if you've reached the objective or not.

Time specific objectives give a deadline to aim for.

SMART

Agreed objectives aren't just handed down from on high. Everyone agrees that they're the right objectives.

Realistic objectives are achievable. People don't work towards obviously impossible objectives — there's no point.

You can pick up big marks by evaluating business objectives in your exam case study — say whether they're SMART or not.

An **example** of a **SMART** objective would be "to increase market share from 13% to 18% within 5 years". It's specific, it's measurable, hopefully it's been agreed by staff, it seems realistic and doable, and it's time specific.

Survival, Profit and Growth are the most Popular Objectives

1) **Survival** is the most important objective during **recession** and when businesses are **starting up**. A lot of new businesses fail within 12 months. Most new businesses experience cash flow problems early on and have to **fight** to survive. Once a firm becomes established and financially strong **other objectives** may become more important.

2) **Profit maximisation** is a **major** objective for established businesses. Firms pursuing profit have to **plan long-term** to get it right — for example, a simple price rise might increase profits in the short term but actually reduce profits in the longer term because higher prices reduce demand. The best way to make profits is to **add value** to the good or service you're selling.

3) Many businesses generate **enough profits** to please their **shareholders** — but hold back from full-on profit maximisation so they can **spend** money to achieve **other objectives**.

4) **Growth** is another key objective for established businesses. Growth helps give job security and creates opportunities for promotion. Shareholders like growth — it makes **hostile takeovers** less likely, it can improve profits through **economies of scale** and it's a sign of **success**.

5) Other objectives might include getting the biggest **market share** possible, being **environmentally friendly**, and putting across the right **corporate image**. Charities and public sector organisations exist to **provide a service to the community**, and that's reflected in their objectives.

In the real world, businesses usually go for a **combination** of objectives. The exact mix depends on the **corporate culture** and **values** of the business, and on the **power** of various groups of **stakeholders**.

Practice Questions

Q1   Give a description and an example of:
   a) a corporate aim, b) a strategic objective, c) an operational objective and d) an individual objective.

Q2   State and explain two reasons why a business might develop a mission statement.

Q3   Explain why a firm should involve staff from all levels when developing a mission statement.

Exam Questions

Q1   Profit maximisation is the only real corporate objective. To what extent do you agree with this view?   (10 marks)

Q2   Analyse the value of a corporate mission statement for a rapidly growing business.   (8 marks)

Our mission is... to Mars. We'll decide what to do when we get there...

You'd be forgiven for thinking all these aims, objectives, strategies and targets are a complicated way of talking about what a firm wants to achieve. The thing is, with a big business you've got your Big Goals (e.g. make profit) and then you've got to set little goals to meet on the way to reaching your Big Goal. Aims are Big Goals, objectives are little goals.

Setting Objectives

Here's more about objectives, and how they're used to make decisions, measure performance and motivate people. **These two pages are for AQA, OCR and Edexcel.**

Objectives *govern* Decision-making *and set* Strategies

Business decisions have to **fit in** with corporate **objectives**. If they don't, there's **no point** in having objectives at all.

1) **Long-term corporate objectives** set the whole **direction** of a business. They affect the **big decisions** that senior managers make. They also govern the setting of operational objectives.

2) **Operational objectives** rule decision-making on the "shop floor" where the **actual work** is done.

Managers can check that **potential** decisions fit with the objective **before** they actually go ahead with a firm decision. They don't have to wait to see if their decision was really the right thing to do. (Of course, managers still make mistakes, and make decisions which turn out not to fit in with their objectives.)

In the exam, if you're asked to evaluate business decisions, make sure you take note of the firm's objectives. Remember that if the objectives are vague and useless, they won't be able to make decisions that push the business in a clear direction.

A **strategy** is a **plan** for how to achieve objectives.
A strategy plans out the **tactics** that a business is going to use to reach its goals.
Tactics are the **actual activities** that the business uses to **work towards** its objectives.

Businesses can have Short-term *and* Long-term Objectives —— *AQA & OCR*

Long-term objectives include things like long-term growth. A long-term growth objective means that managers make **decisions** that aim towards growth. They try to **expand** into new markets, push for **market penetration**, and invest in new product **development**.

Short-term objectives include things like short-term **survival** and making short-term **profit.**

There should be a **balance** between short-term and long-term objectives.

Short-term Objectives — Businesses Can Lose Out in the Long Run

1) **Short-term objectives** usually need a business to **cut back** on all its long-term objectives.

2) For example, a business going hell for leather to increase on last year's profits might **cut** its **advertising** budget, stop its **training** programme, and cut back on its **product development** budget. At the end of the year it'd have **more profit** because of doing away with all those **costs**. But it would have lost out on its other objectives — it'd be in a weaker market position, have less well-trained staff, and it'd be behind on product development.

3) Businesses are often **criticised** for being too concerned with **short-term gain**. UK businesses get a lot of their finance from shareholders, especially banks and pension funds. Banks and pension fund managers want a **quick return** on their investment, or they'll take their money and go elsewhere. Businesses have to go for short-term profits or risk losing investors.

Crisis Management — Reacting to Sudden Changes

1) Businesses have to **switch** to **temporary short-term objectives** to cope with short-term crisis situations.

2) For example, a growth objective might cause **overtrading** and a cash flow crisis (see p.38) — not enough liquid assets available to pay the bills. In a **cash flow crisis**, a business should focus on **short-term survival** instead of medium-term expansion — managers need to find ways of improving cash flow, or the business will go under.

3) For another example, a business going for **profit maximisation** must be prepared to take a **temporary loss of profits** and invest heavily in **advertising** and **promotions** if a new competitor enters the market.

To be successful over a long period, businesses need to **balance** their **overall objectives** with an ability to **react** to a **changing** market place.

If you're asked in the exam about a firm's objectives, check whether the question mentions long-term or short-term rewards. Objectives that suit long-term goals like brand development won't help solve a short-term crisis.

—— *AQA & OCR* ——   —— *AQA & OCR* ——

Setting Objectives

Objectives are useful for Motivating and Measuring Performance

1) **Corporate objectives** let employees know what the **whole firm** is aiming for. They give employees an idea of the **culture** of the business. **Tactical** objectives for each department, operational team and individual worker give employees a **clear idea** of what they're supposed to do. Knowing **exactly** what you have to do (and having a target to aim for) can be **motivating**.

2) It's very important to **communicate** objectives to **everyone** in an organisation, to make sure that everyone knows what they're aiming for.

3) Objectives that **aren't reachable** and are **imposed** on employees by upper management can end up being **seriously demotivating**.

4) **Management by objectives** sets objectives for all departments and individual employees, and **measures performance** according to whether targets are reached or not. There's more about management by objectives on p.62.

Objectives can be Too Fixed — and Stop firms from Reacting to Changes

1) You know that solid objectives give a business something to **aim** for, and that can be a very good thing.

2) However, **fixed objectives** can **stop** a business from reacting quickly to **changes** in the marketplace.

3) The market seems to be changing **faster and faster** these days. Objectives can quickly become **out-of-date**.

4) Some modern management experts think that being able to **respond quickly** is becoming **more important** than sticking to firm objectives.

Objectives can either Minimise Risk or Maximise Reward

1) If you want to win big, you have to take chances. Objectives and strategies that go for **high rewards** are usually the most **risky**. You need a **balance** between low-risk, low-reward strategies and high-risk, high-reward strategies.

2) Some businesses choose to go **all out** for high **profits**, or high **growth**. They're willing to take a **gamble** in the hope of getting big gains. Other businesses choose to **play it safe**, and avoid the risk of making a loss.

3) Risk-taking is related to **business ownership**. Businesses where the owners have **unlimited liability** might shy away from taking big risks. If it all goes wrong, the owners are stuck with all the debts. Incorporated companies with **limited liability** have less to lose. They can take more **risky** actions and bring in higher rewards.

4) Managers in companies where the owners **aren't** the people who **run** the company (where there's "divorce of ownership and control", see p.6) can easily end up setting objectives, making decisions and following strategies that are in their **own interest**, instead of in the interest of the **owners** of the company.

Practice Questions

Q1 What's the difference between an objective and a strategy?
Q2 Explain why a firm might follow short-term objectives which conflict with its long-term corporate objectives.
Q3 Give three benefits to a business of setting objectives.

Exam Question

Q1 The directors of Durrant Jones Ltd are discussing whether to turn the business into a public limited company. Some directors are concerned that being a PLC will force them to focus on short-term profit.
(a) Why might Durrant Jones have to focus on short-term objectives instead of long-term ones? (3 marks)
(b) What effect might a focus on short-term profit have on the business? (9 marks)

Objectives are like, your destination, man...

This objective-strategy-decision thing? Look at it this way — imagine you're driving from Birmingham to Glasgow. You need directions to tell you how to get to Glasgow, and you need to make sure you take the right exit on the motorway and avoid taking wrong turns. A short-term objective of really needing a pee would be met by pulling off into a service station.

Stakeholder Conflicts

*Stakeholders are the people with an interest in how a business performs. Businesses can set objectives to please stakeholders. **These two pages are for AQA, OCR and Edexcel.***

Stakeholders have an Interest in the Wellbeing of a Company

By encouraging **everyone** connected to the business to have an interest in its long-term profitability, a business is likely to have a more secure future. These are the stakeholders in a typical company and some of their interests:

1) Employees want **good wages**. They want **job security** and good job **prospects**. They like work to be local, regular and continuous, with **good hours** to fit in with home life. Employees like extras such as **training** courses, a **pension**, **holiday** allowance and pay, **health care** and **shares** in the company. They want a nice **work environment** and good communication with co-workers. **Managers** want more of the same things as workers — higher pay, more shares, good job prospects and status by association with a successful firm.

2) **Shareholders** (owners) want **short-term profit** and regular **dividend** payments. They want **long-term growth** and they like the company to have a positive **image**.

   This all comes up briefly on p.2, but you need to know it in detail for this part of the syllabus.

3) **Creditors** (suppliers) want **profit** so the company can pay on time. They want **long-term growth** so there are long-term orders which give **stability**. Suppliers like to improve their status by **association** with a successful firm (this is called the **halo effect**).

4) **Customers** want **low prices**, high **quality**, and a good brand **image**. They want goods and services to be easily available. Customers want businesses to have a long-term future (so spares will be available for a long time).

5) The **local population** want jobs. They also want **trade for other businesses** from employees spending their wages locally. They want **sponsorship** of local amenities, sports teams and events. They want **no pollution** — no noise, no fumes, no traffic jams, nothing unsightly.

6) The **state** and the **government** want **growth** in the economy to create jobs — this cuts government costs. They want plenty of **profits** to raise government income from **taxes**. They also like to have a **good skill base** from employee training. **Exports** of high quality goods raise awareness of the country as a brand, and help with the **balance of trade**. The government wants all the **other stakeholders** to be happy, too — a good economy and happy stakeholders makes the **government look good** so they'll be **re-elected**.

A person can belong to **several stakeholder groups** at the same time. For instance, a worker at MG Rover cars is an **employee**. They can also be a shareholder, a local resident, a manager and a customer.

Everyone can benefit with a Stakeholder Approach to business

1) The **stakeholder approach** says that a business should take the needs of **all** its stakeholders into account when making decisions and **setting objectives**. The idea of stakeholders has always been around to some degree. Since the **1980s** it's emerged as a popular way of thinking about setting objectives and making decisions.

2) Everyone is **selfish** to a certain extent — if **you** can **personally gain** something by making sure that the company you work for stays profitable then you're more **motivated** towards that goal. The stakeholder approach gets all stakeholders working in their **own interest** — because they **all** get something out of keeping the business **growing** and **profitable**.

3) Giving stakeholders what they want can **help** the business. For example, paying suppliers on time **motivates** them to provide good quality materials — it helps build a **mutually satisfying business relationship**. Doing things to help the local community can **motivate** local people to go and work at the business.

4) Looking after stakeholders can help the **public image** of the business. A good public image makes it easier for the business to **recruit staff**, raise **finance** from investors and **retain customers**.

The shareholder approach:

1) The stakeholder approach is in contrast to the shareholder approach. The shareholder concept says that each business is only accountable to its owners — its shareholders.

2) It's a simpler idea than the stakeholder concept — but businesses can lose out by not taking the specific interests of employees, customers, suppliers and the community into account.

Stakeholder Conflicts

Stakeholder Conflicts — you can't please everyone

1) The needs and wants of different stakeholder groups aren't always **compatible** with each other. Each group of stakeholders tends to concentrate on its **own interests** and want things done its own way.

2) The main balance when making big decisions is between **short-term profit** and **social responsibility**.

Profit is important

1) Without pushing to produce a profit the company will be unable to survive. It won't be able to pay its **suppliers** or its **employees** — that's two major stakeholders right up the spout.

2) **Shareholders** need profit so that they can get their dividends. Shareholders may decide to sack the directors or sell their shares to someone else, if they aren't getting enough return.

Social responsibility is also important

1) Companies that ignore their social responsibilities can face problems. E.g. Polluting the local environment could **put consumers off**. The state may intervene with legislation to close down production at factories which cause the worst pollution.

2) A decision to relocate production to another country with cheaper labour wouldn't be seen as socially responsible or patriotic. The state can intervene with incentives that cut the cost of staying in the UK — subsidised land and buildings, tax breaks and so on.

The **importance** that a company gives to a particular stakeholder group in a given situation depends upon the **effect** of the **actions** of the stakeholder group. For instance, employees may decide to go on **strike** if the company increases their working hours to meet production targets. Striking makes their demand more **important** to the business.

People have different demands and interests, depending upon which stakeholder group they belong to. The company must try to satisfy as **many** groups as possible and **still survive financially**. It's not easy, but businesses manage it.

Stakeholders **don't always disagree** — for example, making workers happy can actually help productivity and raise profits. Remember this if you get asked to "evaluate the extent to which stakeholder groups have conflicting needs".

Resolving stakeholder conflicts calls for Good Communication

1) Stakeholder conflicts are **worst** when one group of stakeholders feels that they're being **ignored** by the business, and that the business doesn't care about their needs.

2) Businesses can avoid the worst stakeholder conflicts by **listening** to stakeholder needs. Even if they don't necessarily do what stakeholders want, it helps.

3) Big businesses today often mention their stakeholders in their **mission statement** — they make it part of their **corporate aim** to keep their stakeholders **sweet**. Mission statements often mention things like **environmental** responsibility, **customer** needs, giving something back to local **communities** and giving **employees** a nice workplace and the potential for a fulfilling job.

Practice Questions

Q1 What is a stakeholder?

Q2 Name a stakeholder group. What are the main interests of that group?

Q3 Give an example of a person who belongs to more than one group of stakeholders.

Q4 Why do conflicts between stakeholders arise?

Exam Questions

Q1 A computer manufacturer decides to open a new production facility in the UK. Discuss the effect this new facility will have on the various stakeholders in the company. (10 marks)

Q2 Describe how a stakeholder conflict might occur when employees demand a 10% wage increase. (4 marks)

Profits — *and* bunnies and flowers and candy floss and fluffy clouds and...

OK, so now you know about the stakeholder concept and how it's used to push companies forward and make them more profitable. You need to understand the point of view of each stakeholder group — this'll make it easy to describe, analyse and evaluate the conflicts which come up. In the exam, make sure your answer's relevant to the business in the question.

SWOT Analysis

Businesses analyse their situation before deciding on their strategy. **These two pages are for OCR and AQA.**

Good Strategies make the Most of the Situation

Business **strategies** and **tactics** depend on the **resources** that a business has, and the **conditions** "out there" in the market. Businesses need to do plenty of **analysis** before they finally decide their strategies.

> **Rules for a great business strategy — internal factors**
>
> 1) A strategy should make the **most** of a firm's **strengths**.
> 2) It should make sure that the **weaknesses** of the firm have as **little impact** as possible on business.

> **Rules for a great business strategy — external factors**
>
> 1) It should look for **gaps** in the market, and try to fill them.
> 2) It should watch out for what **competitors** are doing.
> 3) It should take account of what's going on in the **economy**, and any new **laws** that the government might be planning to make.

SWOT analysis looks at Strengths, Weaknesses, Opportunities and Threats

SWOT actually stands for <u>S</u>trengths, <u>W</u>eaknesses, <u>O</u>pportunities and <u>T</u>hreats, which makes it easy to remember.

> **STRENGTHS** are **internal factors**. They include things like a good **range of products**, a skilled and motivated **workforce**, a well known **brand** name, and a good **distribution network**.

> **WEAKNESSES** are also **internal factors**. They include things like not enough **capital** for expansion and new equipment, not having enough **new products**, an **inexperienced** workforce, high distribution **costs** (e.g. lots of high street shops, no mail order or e-business), having a lot of **debts**.

> **OPPORTUNITIES** are **external factors** that create the **potential** for a business to develop and do better. They include things like an improving economic climate which would create more demand. New overseas markets can open up because of political changes, or because of economic development abroad. They give opportunities to sell goods to a new market, and to buy materials from cheap overseas suppliers.

> **THREATS** are **external factors** that make it **harder** for the business to succeed. A growing number of competitors in the market is a threat. New laws such as health and safety regulations can be limiting and costly. Environmental worries can make consumers look for "greener" products. Economic factors such as a high pound/euro exchange rate can be a threat (see p.97).

> Remember — strengths and opportunities aren't the same thing. Strengths are good things <u>inside</u> the business. Opportunities are factors <u>outside</u> the business that give it a chance to do really well. Same thing with weaknesses and threats. Weaknesses are inside the business, threats come from outside.

External opportunities and threats Change over time

1) The **economic climate** has a direct influence on business. Interest rates, inflation and unemployment all affect business. A **feel-good** atmosphere in the economy encourages consumers to buy more. The economic climate changes over time. Governments and central banks tweak the economy to get it performing better.

2) **Politics** affects business. When **governments change**, they bring in different economic policies. Governments introduce **laws** which affect businesses — new tax rules, consumer protection laws, employment laws etc.

3) **Social trends** affect business. Health concerns and environmental concerns can affect demand. Also, fashion changes and changes in the age distribution of the population affect demand for some goods and services.

4) **New technology** has a direct effect on demand for some products, e.g. new-generation mobile phones — as soon as you can make a good video cameraphone, people will rush to get one.

SWOT Analysis

SWOT analysis Helps Managers see what's up

1) SWOT analysis helps managers see **exactly** where the business is **right now**.

2) It also looks at the **external environment** and helps managers see **opportunities** for success and **threats** to success — both **now** and coming up in the **near future**.

3) SWOT analysis forces managers to take a **long hard look** at the business. If they didn't do this, it'd be easy to bumble along thinking everything's just fine — until a major **crisis** happens.

4) By looking at the opportunities and threats coming up in the **near future**, a business can **take action** to make the **most** of the opportunities and **avoid** being damaged by the threats.

Example:	**A clothing retailer thinking about diversifying into homewares (cushions, crockery, cutlery etc).**
Strengths:	A strong brand name in clothing, existing outlets and distribution network, good employees.
Weaknesses:	Lack of experience in the homewares market. Employees lack product knowledge.
Opportunities:	Potential for increased sales, potential to spread risk across more product lines, potential for stronger seasonal sales in the run up to Christmas as people buy more homewares than clothes as gifts.
Threats:	Several large well-established competitors selling at low prices.

Without doing a SWOT analysis, managers might get carried away thinking how easy it would be to start selling homewares without realising that there are a lot of competitors and it would be hard to undercut them on price.

The SWOT analysis shows the potential for seasonal sales.

SWOT analysis has its own Weaknesses

Nothing's perfect in this life, including SWOT analysis.

One problem is that SWOT analysis only gives you the **facts** about strengths, weaknesses, opportunities and threats. It doesn't tell you what strategy to use. It doesn't **tell you** what **tactics** to use to put your strategy into practice.

Another big problem is that SWOT analysis requires managers to be totally **upfront** and **honest** with themselves. It's easy to **overstate** all the **good** things about the business and the market, and **understate** all the **bad** things. This is **dangerous** — playing down a threat or overestimating your ability to deal with it means you aren't fully prepared.

Practice Questions

Q1 How should a business's strategies take account of its strengths and weaknesses?

Q2 List the four areas of a SWOT analysis.

Q3 Which parts of a SWOT analysis relate to internal factors and which relate to external factors?

Exam Questions

Q1 The owner of a small manufacturer of curtain fabric in East Anglia is considering selling her products in the EU. Up to now her company has only sold in the UK. She has a small, hard-working local workforce and her products are of a good quality. Neither she nor her employees have experience of doing business in Europe. The trade magazines she has read indicate she will face stiff competition. However, as the EU is expanding she is convinced the future of her business lies in Europe. Prepare a SWOT analysis for her to discuss with the other directors. (14 marks)

Q2 Explain why a business should draw up a strategy, and outline how a SWOT analysis could assist in this process. (9 marks)

Yes, you're going to SWOT up on this — oh how I wish I was funny...

SWOT analysis isn't too complicated as long as you go through it methodically. It can take a bit of imagination to come up with all the strengths, weaknesses, opportunities and threats of a business and its situation, though. Remember that strengths and opportunities aren't the same thing, and neither are weaknesses and threats.

Starting a Small Firm

Starting a small business is easy, but making a living out of it is hard. The examiners want you to show that you understand that starting a successful small firm is not just about having an idea. **These pages are for AQA, and the bits about entrepreneurs are also useful for Edexcel.**

People who start businesses are called *Entrepreneurs*

The formal definition of an entrepreneur: ⟶ "A person who **organises** the **factors of production** to generate **economic wealth** through business activity."

1) What this posh definition really means is that a person (or a group of people) **raise the resources** and **organise the activities** needed to **start a business**.

2) These factors include financial investment, staff, buildings, research and development, and marketing.

3) If the entrepreneur **organises** things well, and consumers **want** the product or service, the business will succeed. If they get it **wrong** the business will have to give up and stop trading.

Entrepreneurs are *Innovative Risk-takers*, *Planners* and *Organisers*

1) Entrepreneurs are **innovators** who either have an **original idea**, or a way of **adapting** an existing idea to make it **different** from the competition, e.g. selling goods at lower prices to a new segment of the market.

2) They have **perseverance**. James Dyson took twenty years to get his new design of vacuum cleaner to the market because he couldn't get an existing manufacturer to adopt his ideas. Eventually, he raised the **finance** himself and started his **own small business** to make what's now one of the best-selling cleaners in the world.

3) They're **risk-takers**. When starting a business, many entrepreneurs have to use their **own financial resources** to provide start-up capital. If the business fails, they lose their investment. They're **prepared** to take the risk.

4) They're **planners**. Entrepreneurs plan what financial, technical and human resources they'll need.

5) They're **good organisers** and organise resources so that they're used cost effectively.

Entrepreneurs research *Profitable Business Opportunities*

1) Before starting a new business, successful entrepreneurs may have several ideas but they won't **commit** large resources until they feel confident that the chosen idea will **work**.

2) They need to be confident that there's enough **demand** for the product or service.

3) They also need to be sure that they have the **skills** to provide the product or service.

4) Entrepreneurs need to figure out how much money they'll make. It's only worth going ahead with a business idea if it's **profitable** — if the **income** will **cover the costs**.

5) A new business won't attract customers unless it can offer something different — a **unique selling point**. This could be quality, low price, good customer service etc.

6) It's really important to get the **price** right. If the price is too high, sales will be too low to make enough money. If the price is too low, the total revenue won't be enough.

Original *Ideas* are business *Assets* that can be *Protected* by law

Businesses and individuals who produce **original work** and earn an income through it need to **protect their ideas** from being copied by others. The protection can be achieved in several ways.

1) A **patent** is a way of **registering** and **protecting** a new invention. Patents are granted by the **Patent Office**, a government agency that checks that an invention such as a machine, or even a can ring-pull, is an original design. If you have a patent for your **product**, or your **method** for producing it, no one else can copy it unless you give them a **licence** — and you can **charge** for the licence.

2) **Trademarks** protect logos and slogans etc. The design of the McDonald's golden arches logo is the **intellectual property** of the McDonald's Corporation and it can't be used by any other company. McDonald's promote a certain **brand image** — if the logo was used by other companies, McDonald's **reputation** might be damaged.

3) **Copyright** gives protection to **written work** and **music**. Authors and musicians or their publishers receive **royalties** every time their work is published or played on the radio.

Starting a Small Firm

Market Research must be Cost Effective on a Small Budget

1) Before start-up, it's important to get to know the **market**. The entrepreneur should be aware of the social, environmental, legal and economic factors that can limit how they can market their product.

2) **Professional market research** can be very expensive. New small businesses don't have a lot of money to spend on research, so they have to do it themselves.

3) New businesses can easily do **secondary research** on a **small budget**. They can look at articles in newspapers. They can get information from **Companies House** about the profits or losses of other businesses in the same market. Large reference libraries and local business support organisations can access data on different market sectors. Information can also be found on the **Internet**.

4) Small businesses can also do low-budget **primary market research**. This may take the form of a **questionnaire** asking potential customers their opinions of the idea, or **observation** of activities in a similar business.

5) It's really important to be **objective** and **scientific** when doing your own primary research. It's easy and tempting to ask **loaded questions** that tend to lead people into giving the answer you want. It's easy to ask **friends** and **family** who give "nice" answers out of politeness. Watch out for this in exam questions — the new business owner in the case study may have done **unreliable** market research. You'd be spot-on to **question** their methods and their findings.

6) There's only one thing **worse** than well-meaning but unreliable market research, and that's **no market research** at all. Bizarrely enough, some people **don't bother** to do any market research before starting a business. They think it's a waste of money, and prefer to spend their **limited cash** on fine-tuning the product. They don't stand much chance of getting the product right if they **don't know** whether or not it's really what the market **wants**.

> It's best to do market research **before** finalising the details of the product or service. People starting a new business can learn an awful lot from market research, and may find that they have to seriously **adapt** and **develop** their original idea to make it **fit in** with what the market **needs**.

Marketing must be Cost Effective too

1) At the start, a new business doesn't have oodles of money to spend on **advertising** campaigns. As far as **above-the-line** promotion goes, ads in the **local paper** and a few cheaply printed **leaflets** shoved through doors are going to be the limit.

2) **Below-the-line promotions** can be **cheap** to organise. New businesses can do special offers like "buy five, get the sixth free" to get people buying.

3) It's important to not stimulate demand **too much** — when demand is greater than the **capacity** of the business, the business has to turn customers away, which isn't good for customer relations, to say the least...

Practice Questions

Q1 Give three personal characteristics of a successful entrepreneur.

Q2 Why is it important to get the price of a product right?

Q3 What is a patent for?

Q4 What's the main danger of doing your own market research?

Exam Questions

Q1 Explain how the personal characteristics of a successful entrepreneur will help a new business start-up to become successful. (10 marks)

Q2 Johan Möller has invented a new salad spinner, and he is setting up his own business to make and sell it.
(a) Outline two difficulties that Johan will face in setting up his business. (4 marks)
(b) Outline two benefits that Johan will get from patenting his idea. (4 marks)

All you need is an idea... and lots of research... and the right attitude...

Starting a new business sounds like a great idea — you get to be your own boss, and hopefully make scads of money to spend on fast cars and bling. But it can be scary — there are an awful lot of things to be responsible for. It seems that entrepreneurs have to do a heck of a lot of leg work to find out what the market's like and what they need to do to succeed.

Starting a Small Firm

Once the entrepreneur has done research to make sure their product or service is right for the market, they need to get into the nuts and bolts of actually setting up a working business, and making sure it keeps going. **For AQA only.**

All Start-Ups *present the same practical* Problems *for entrepreneurs*

The steps that have to be taken when starting a new firm are common to all businesses.

1) Entrepreneurs need to prepare a business plan to explain in detail their ideas and business objectives.
2) All entrepreneurs need to decide how to raise finance in the most cost-effective way.
3) They also have to plan the cash flow during the start-up period.
4) They have to decide the best location for the business so that it suits the market where it'll trade.
5) Next, they need to devise a strategy to build a customer base which will provide a steady flow of revenue.

Before starting a new business, the owner chooses a legal structure. Owners of small firms usually choose to become sole traders, partnerships or private limited companies because they're relatively easy to set up. See Section One, especially p.4-7, for more on this.

A Business Plan *is* Essential *if a new business start-up is to* Succeed

1) A **business plan** is a document that states **what** the owner(s) want to do and **how** they intend to do it.
2) It **reminds** the owner of the **ideas** they had before the business started.
3) It **informs** any **lenders** or **investors** who may want to help finance the start-up. **Banks** and **venture capitalists** demand a properly thought out business plan before they'll think about investing.
4) The plan gives details of the **business objectives**, including the **type of market** in which the business will trade, the **expected profits** and the **time** it's expected to take before the business reaches its full profit level.
5) The business plan includes information on the **structure** of the market, who the main **competitors** are, where the business intends to position itself in the market, and what the **unique selling point** is. The plan will also include details of any **market research** that the owner's done.
6) **Estimates** of costs, sales, and revenue give **investors**, including the owner, something to compare progress with during the start-up period. The figures are usually shown in a **table** and must be **realistic**. The financial information will need to explain **how** the business will **survive** in the start-up period.

Raising Finance *for a new small business needs* Top Negotiating Skills

Investing in a new business can be very **risky** for the investor — they need to **trust** that the business will succeed. Entrepreneurs need to do everything they can to **win the trust** of the investor. Having a good **business plan** helps. Wearing a **nice suit** helps. Being a good **negotiator** really helps.

There are several sources of finance that the new business owner can access:

1) Investing the owner's **personal savings**. Some entrepreneurs use **redundancy payments** or **remortgage** their houses. Sometimes a **partnership** arrangement is the answer.
2) It can be difficult to **borrow** money for a new business from the bank — banks need to be **convinced** that the idea is a good one. **Interest rates** are **higher** for new businesses than for established ones with a proven track record — this is to **reduce** the **risk** of investing in a new business.
3) Venture capitalists or **"Business Angels"** are established companies who give financial **support** to new companies if they can be **convinced** that the business idea is original and has the potential to be successful. In return, they're entitled to share in the **profits** of the company for a limited period of time, e.g. five years.
4) **Local authorities** don't provide start-up capital, but they may have business units available at **low rents** to new businesses. This helps by **reducing the finance** that a business will need to get started.

For this section, you really need to know about sources of finance for different types of business ownership — and focus on how new business owners find money, not how established businesses find money.

New businesses *must have enough* Cash Flow *to cover the* Start-up Period

1) Cash flow always goes up and down. See p.38 for the cash flow cycle.
2) In a new business there's an extra time lag. Even with careful cost management, the business has to **spend** on stock, fixed assets and marketing **before** customers pay for the goods or services provided.

Starting a Small Firm

Location depends on the Type of Goods or Services provided

1) Some businesses must be **close** to their **customers**. If customers have to visit the business premises, e.g. if it's a shoe shop or a dentist's surgery, this is the most important factor.

2) **Manufacturing** or **processing** businesses are often located in areas where raw materials are found. This cuts down on transport costs.

3) Some small businesses can be where the **owner lives**. Self-employed consultants can easily work from home, thanks to **communication technology** like the Internet and email.

4) Some businesses absolutely have to be near good **transport** links. Roads, rail and air facilities are important to all small businesses who sell goods and services over a wide area.

5) Being in a **Regional Aid Area** can help. In poorer areas of the country, new business start-ups can get **grants** and **tax breaks** from the **government** and the **European Union**.

Getting and Keeping Customers is Essential to business success

1) New business owners who have set up on their own after being **employed** in the same **industry** can get custom from people who **knew** them in their previous job. For example, if a chiropodist working in a partnership decides to set up as a sole trader, some of her **existing clients** will go to her **new business** for foot treatment, instead of going to the place where she used to work.

2) New business owners without existing clients have to rely on **advertising**, **mailshots** or **canvassing** over the phone. These methods can take a lot of time and effort. It's hard to convince people to change their **buying habits**.

3) The best method of getting and keeping customers is to build a **good reputation** through **customer service**. This attracts **repeat business** — customers keep coming back. They **recommend** the business to their friends, too. Repeat business and word of mouth recommendations are a cheap and effective way to win sales.

40% of Small Businesses Fail within the First Three Years of starting up

These business failures happen for some of the following reasons:

1) **Poor** or nonexistent **market research**.

2) **Insufficient capital invested** to cover start-up expenses such as equipment.

3) **Low working capital** while the business finds customers and buys raw materials.

4) General **economic** conditions becoming **unfavourable**, e.g. rising interest rates increase the cost of borrowing, and high unemployment means fewer customers.

Practice Questions

Q1 What steps do all entrepreneurs have to take before starting up a business?

Q2 What is a business plan?

Q3 What would you expect a business plan to contain?

Q4 Give five factors that can influence the location of a new business.

Q5 What low-cost marketing techniques could the owner of a new small business use to establish a customer base?

Exam Questions

Q1 Discuss how a business plan can help a new small business start-up to succeed. (7 marks)

Q2 Describe and evaluate ways an entrepreneur can raise finance to fund a new small firm. (8 marks)

Dude... starting up a new business is like, really hard...

There really is a lot more to starting a business than I'd have thought at first — writing a business plan, getting money, getting customers and then running the business. Loads of new businesses start each year and many of them succeed. The ones that fail often fail because the owner didn't do market research, or didn't manage the finances properly.

Markets and Competition

Businesses operate in a market economy, influenced by supply and demand. The kind of market and the level of competition in the market affect what the business does. **These two pages are for AQA, OCR and Edexcel.**

Market Forces *of* Supply *and* Demand *determine* Price *and* Quantity *in markets*

1) In a market, **buyers demand** and **sellers supply** — with rival sellers **competing** to sell their goods. Competition encourages firms to be **efficient** and keep prices low. It also increases **choice** for consumers.

2) **Demand** is the quantity that buyers will **buy** at a particular price. Demand goes **up** as **price** goes **down**, and vice versa.

3) **Supply** is the quantity that sellers will **put out for sale** at a particular price. Supply goes **up** as **price** goes **up**, and vice versa.

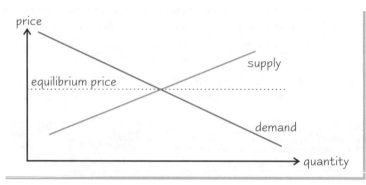

4) In a **free market**, the **market forces** of demand and supply determine the **equilibrium price**. The equilibrium price is the price where the **quantity demanded** is equal to the **quantity supplied**.

5) When there's excess demand or excess supply, the market is in **disequilibrium** — out of balance. Markets in disequilibrium move **back towards equilibrium**. What this means is that when the price is too high, excess supply makes sellers cut prices to increase demand. When the price is too low, there's **too much demand** for a limited supply so buyers will be willing to pay more and the **price rises** back to the equilibrium level.

6) Excess demand in the market is also called **capacity shortage** — there isn't enough **capacity** in the market to meet demand. When there's a capacity shortage, **prices go up**, existing producers **invest** in more equipment so they can **produce more**, **new producers** try to get into the market, and customers look to buy from **abroad**.

7) Excess supply is also called **excess capacity** or **spare capacity**. When a business has spare capacity that it isn't using, it can try to sell in **new markets**, or use its capacity to **produce other things**. It can also **sell off** production facilities to **reduce** production capacity. There's more about **capacity utilisation** on p.70-71.

You need to be able to Calculate Elasticity of Demand
— Edexcel —

1) Demand responds to changes in price. Price elasticity of demand shows how much demand changes in response to changes in price.

Price elasticity of demand = $\dfrac{\textbf{\% change in quantity demanded}}{\textbf{\% change in price}}$

Products with a big change in demand in response to a small change in price are price elastic. Products where the demand doesn't change much, even when the price goes up and down a lot, are price inelastic.

> There's more about elasticity of demand on p.30-31.

2) Demand responds to changes in income. Income elasticity of demand shows how much price changes in response to changes in income.

Income elasticity of demand = $\dfrac{\textbf{\% change in quantity demanded}}{\textbf{\% change in real incomes}}$

Most goods have **positive** income elasticity of demand — as income rises, the demand rises. However, inferior goods (i.e. low quality, cheap products) have **negative** income elasticity of demand — **demand falls** when **income rises** and **rises** when **income falls**.

> Change in <u>real income</u> means change in income taking <u>inflation</u> (see p.96) into account — that is, it's the increase or decrease in your capacity to <u>buy stuff</u>.

3) Cross elasticity of demand says whether two goods are complements or substitutes. **Complements** are goods which **go together**, e.g. tennis balls and tennis rackets. **Substitutes** are goods which are **alternatives** to each other, like butter and margarine.

Cross elasticity of demand = $\dfrac{\textbf{\% change in demand for product A}}{\textbf{\% change in price of product B}}$

Cross elasticity for complementary goods is negative — if the price of **tennis balls** goes **up**, **demand** for **rackets falls**.
Cross elasticity for **substitutes** is positive – when the **price of one rises**, **demand for the other rises**.

— Edexcel —   — Edexcel —

Vertical side labels: Edexcel (left), Edexcel (right)

Markets and Competition

Different **Market Structures** have **Varying Degrees** of **Competition**

Features of a monopoly

A monopoly is where **one business** has **complete control** over the market. There's **no competition**. There are **no alternatives** to the product, so consumers must buy at the price offered by the monopoly. Monopolies have **complete market power**. The Competition Commission in the UK stops businesses from creating a monopoly.

Features of a very competitive market

Markets where products or services sold by different businesses are very **similar** (e.g. petrol) are **highly competitive**. Consumers shop around based on **price**. In a hypothetical **perfect competition** market, there'd be no **barriers to entry**. In the real world, there are always some barriers to entry.

Barriers to entry are obstacles preventing new firms entering a market. Examples are high start-up costs, control over possible outlets, patents and trademarks, and legal requirements.

Features of a market with many small firms

Markets with lots of small businesses won't always be highly competitive. Small businesses often try to get into a **niche market** — a market that wants to buy a **specialised, differentiated service** that they provide. **Hairdressers** and **restaurants** are common examples — a hairdresser may offer a **high standard of haircut**, in a **fashionable** salon with **staff** who make good conversation and a restaurant may have **high quality food** and very **polite waiters**. Consumers make choices according to **personal needs**, not just on price.

Competition can be **Fair** or **Unfair**

1) **Fair competition** in a market is where all businesses compete on an **equal footing**. Fair competition means that customers can get good quality products and services for low prices. Businesses have to compete on quality and price, so the **best quality** and the **lowest prices** end up winning customers.

2) **Cartels** are an example of **unfair competition**. In a cartel, businesses get together to decide how they're going to share out the market, and agree to charge the **same high prices**. This kind of **price fixing** can also happen more informally, without a cartel being formed.

3) **Monopolies** are another example of **unfair competition**.

4) **Predatory pricing** is unfair. It's where a large business sets prices at such a **low level** that smaller competitors cannot compete — if they don't cut their prices they'll lose sales, and if they do cut prices, they'll make a loss.

5) **Powerful businesses** can **bully** retailers into either stocking the full range of their products or not being allowed to stock any of the range. This means that smaller suppliers get squeezed out of the market.

6) In the UK and the European Union, unfair competition is **illegal**. The **Competition Commission** regulates mergers and takeovers. It doesn't allow mergers and takeovers which would create monopolies. See p.99 for more on competition policy and competition law.

Practice Questions

Q1 Give a definition of equilibrium price.

Q2 What happens to price when there's a capacity shortage?

Q3 The price of product S falls by 10%, and as a consequence demand for product T rises by 5%. Are products S and T complements or substitutes?

Q4 What are the main features of a monopoly?

Exam Questions

Q1 Explain, in terms of market equilibrium, why the price of red roses rises around St Valentine's Day. (6 marks)

Q2 In what type of market structure do restaurants operate? Explain your answer. (8 marks)

There's no getting away from market forces...

Market forces are strongest in a free market with lots of competition. Real life markets don't always have perfect competition. Sometimes this is because there's unfair competition in the market which has to be stamped out. It can also be because of product differentiation between sellers — people buy what makes them happy as well as what's cheapest.

Economic Influences

There are lots of ways in which the national economy can affect businesses.
These two pages are for AQA, OCR and Edexcel.

The **National Economy** is an **External Influence** on business

1) **Gross Domestic Product** (GDP) is a measure of **national income** and **output** of goods and services, usually measured over a year.

2) **Economic growth** is an **increase** in an economy's output.

3) Economic growth means more **demand** in the economy, more **output**, the potential for **economies of scale** (see p.68) and more **profit**. Sustained growth increases **confidence** and helps businesses **plan** for the future.

4) There are some arguments **against** economic growth. Growth has **external costs** like pollution. People work more and have less leisure time, so you can argue that people's **quality of life** goes **down**.

5) Things like **inflation** and **interest rates** which affect the whole economy are called **macro-economic** factors.

The **Ups** and **Downs** of the **Economy** are called the **Business Cycle** — OCR & AQA

1) Over time, an economy usually goes through ups and downs. This is called the **business cycle** or **trade cycle**.

2) In a **recovery** or upswing, **production increases**, and **employment** increases. People spend more. More **new businesses** start up. Businesses use up spare capacity to meet demand, and may **invest** in production facilities.

3) In a **boom**, production levels are high. As production reaches **maximum capacity**, there isn't enough capacity to meet demand — which results in **shortages**, and price increases. Shortages of skilled labour mean **wages go up**. High prices and high wages cause **inflation** (see p.96), which ends the boom.

4) In a **recession** incomes start to go down, and **demand** goes down. Businesses **reduce production**. They may **cut jobs**, or cut the **hours** that employees work. Business **confidence** goes down.

5) In a **slump**, production is at a **low**. Businesses close factories and there are a lot of **redundancies**. **Unemployment** is **high**. A lot of businesses become **insolvent** or **bankrupt**.

Firms survive the business cycle by **diversifying** and by producing **necessities**, such as basic foods and petrol, which aren't subject to fluctuating demand. Firms which produce **consumer durables** (like cars and furniture) and firms which produce **luxuries** are hit hard in **recessions** but prosper especially well in **booms**.

If you wanted to be all fancy, you could say that the extent to which a business is affected by change in GDP depends on the <u>income elasticity of demand</u> *of whatever it's producing. See p.31 for more on income elasticity of demand.*

— OCR & AQA — — OCR & AQA —

The **Business Cycle** has **Several Causes** — AQA

1) **Investment decisions** make upturns and downturns **more pronounced** — when demand is rising, firms invest more in fixed assets so that they can produce more. This makes incomes rise and so demand increases even more. Near full capacity, investment falls so incomes and demand fall.

2) **Stockholding** causes falls in demand to be more pronounced. As demand begins to fall off, stocks begin to build up. A business can use these stocks to satisfy demand, so production is cut. This means that incomes — of employees and suppliers, for example — are also cut, and the downswing is reinforced. Then when demand picks up, the business raises production, so raising incomes and reinforcing the upswing. Changes in **production levels affect incomes**, which **affect demand**.

3) Ups and downs in the economy can have **political** causes — before elections, governments try to boost demand so the economy grows and unemployment falls.

Governments try to make the **Business Cycle** go **Slowly** and **Gently**

1) In a **recession**, governments **cut taxes** (see p.98) to make businesses more **confident**, and to give people more **money** to spend. They can also increase **government spending** on benefits, and on building roads and schools.

2) In a **boom**, the government needs to control inflation by reducing demand. They reduce people's spending power by **raising taxes** and **cutting spending**.

These are called counter-cyclical policies.

— AQA — — AQA —

Economic Influences

Interest Rates *significantly influence business*

1) The interest rate is the **reward** offered to savers and the **cost** of **borrowing** money.
For example, if you borrow £100 and pay 5% interest a year, you'll be paying £5 interest a year.

2) **Higher interest rates** mean **less disposable income** (the income you have left after paying taxes, mortgage etc).
This is because **most** people **borrow more** on things like mortgages, credit cards, loans and overdrafts than
they have **saved** in the bank. Because people have less to spend, **demand falls**. High interest rates make the
cost of borrowing higher and they make **savings** more **attractive** than spending, which also reduces demand.
Because it costs more for businesses to borrow money, businesses suffer and **unemployment rises**.

3) **Lower interest rates** mean **more disposable income**. Borrowing is **cheaper**, and **saving** is **less attractive**.
People can borrow money to spend, so **demand rises** and businesses **prosper**. There's an inverse relationship
between interest rates and economic growth — as one rises the other falls.

Relationship between interest rates, spending, demand and unemployment

Interest rates	Disposable income	Consumer spending	Demand in the economy	Economic output	Unemployment
go up ↑	goes down ↓	goes down ↓	goes down ↓	goes down ↓	goes up ↑
go down ↓	goes up ↑	goes up ↑	goes up ↑	goes up ↑	goes down ↓

4) The **effect** that interest rates have on **demand** depends on the
particular good or service, and whether you're likely to need to
borrow money to buy it. Demand for **new cars** is affected a
lot — when interest rates are high, people keep their old car
instead of taking out an **expensive loan** for a new one.

5) Firms' **investment** is also affected by interest rates. When
interest rates are low, investment projects become more
attractive and firms borrow money to invest in fixed assets.

Interest rates are usually set low in periods of **recession** and **slump**, to **encourage spending** and **demand**.
Rates are usually set **higher** in boom times, to **reduce spending** and demand and **slow down** growth — it's better
to have a **slow** period of growth that lasts for years than a big boom followed by a major slump. In the UK,
interest rates are set by the **Monetary Policy Committee** of the **Bank of England** which is politically **independent**.

Interest Rates *affect the* Exchange Rate

When UK interest rates rise, this attracts money for **investment** into the UK from abroad. The demand for
pounds therefore increases, so the exchange rate rises. This makes imports cheaper but UK exports relatively
more expensive on world markets. See p.97 for more about how the exchange rate affects foreign trade.

Practice Questions

Q1 What is GDP?

Q2 What are the phases of the business cycle?

Q3 How does government policy affect businesses?

Q4 Who sets interest rates in the UK?

Exam Questions

Q1 Describe two ways in which an increase in interest rates could affect a large manufacturing company. (10 marks)

Q2 Evaluate the business opportunities that may arise for a large manufacturing company
when the economy enters the recovery phase of the business cycle. (15 marks)

Is your interest rate holding up, or are you starting to get slightly bored...

*Blimey. After all that I almost feel qualified enough to go on the Today programme and talk about the reasons why the Bank
of England's been putting interest rates up. Notice I said "almost". I do feel qualified to write an essay about the business
cycle, counter-cyclical policies and interest rates — which is a good thing, because that's exactly what this page is for.*

Economic Influences

Inflation and unemployment are bad news for business. Changes in the exchange rate can be good or bad news — depending on whether you're importing or exporting. **These pages are for AQA, OCR and Edexcel.**

Inflation is a Sustained Rise in Prices — and Fall in the Value of Money

1) Inflation is measured by the **Consumer Prices Index** (CPI) which lists the prices of hundreds of goods and services which the average household would buy.

2) There's always **some** inflation. At the moment it's **very low** — roughly 2%. Various things can make inflation **go up**.

The CPI includes mortgage payments. Taking out mortgage payments gives the underlying rate of inflation. Leaving them in gives the headline rate of inflation.

3) High inflation can be caused by **too much demand** in the economy — more than the economy can supply. This is called **demand-pull** inflation. Excess demand when the economy is near its full capacity is called **overheating**.

4) Rises in inflation can be caused by **rising costs** pushing up **prices** — this is called **cost-push** inflation. **Wage rises** can cause prices to go up — especially if productivity isn't rising, because firms have to put prices up to **cover** increased wage costs.

5) **Expectations** of inflation can make inflation worse. A business which expects its **suppliers** to put their prices up will put its **own** prices up to cover increased costs. Employees' expectations of rising prices makes them demand **higher wages**, which makes prices go up. This is the **wage-price spiral** — it's a big cause of cost-push inflation.

6) Inflation can have **serious economic effects**. The faster and higher the inflation, the worse the effects are.

- **Spending goes up temporarily** — people **rush to buy more** before prices go up even more. But then if wages don't go up in line with inflation, sales go down as people can afford less. Sales don't go down as much with **demand-pull** inflation — demand-pull inflation happens **because** there's high demand.
- Inflation causes **uncertainty** and makes it hard for businesses to **plan ahead**. This makes them **invest less**.
- Inflation can be **good for borrowing** money and **bad for lending** money — loans are worth more when you get them than they are when you have to repay them.
- **Cost-push** inflation makes **profit margins** go **down** if businesses decide not to put up their prices.
- **Demand-pull** inflation can actually make **profit margins** go **up**. Businesses operating at or near full capacity can put up prices in response to **high demand** without their **costs** going up by as much.
- Workers with **good bargaining power** can make their earnings **keep up** with inflation. Workers with **poor** bargaining power **lose out**. Their income isn't **worth** as much in terms of what it can buy.
- Inflation in the UK makes UK **exports** expensive abroad. UK businesses become **less competitive**.

7) The impact of inflation depends on **how high** inflation is, what's **causing** it and how high inflation is in **other countries**. Read exam questions about inflation carefully before you launch into an answer.

8) **Deflation** is the **opposite** of inflation — it's when prices keep going down. Deflation happens when there's **too much supply**, or when there's very **high unemployment**. It's **rare** these days.

Unemployment is a Waste of Labour Resources

1) There are different types of unemployment:

Structural unemployment is due to changes in the structure of the economy, e.g. a **decline** in a **major industry** like coal mining. Structural unemployment is often concentrated in particular regions of the country.

Frictional unemployment is temporary, and caused by the **delay** between **losing** one job and **finding** another.

Cyclical unemployment is due to the **downturn** in the business cycle, i.e. a lack of **demand** for labour.

Seasonal unemployment is due to the **season**, e.g. ice cream sellers in the winter.

2) High unemployment can affect **sales**. Producers of **luxury** goods are badly affected by **cyclical** unemployment. Businesses producing **essentials** aren't affected all that much.

3) **Structural** unemployment affects **local** businesses — unemployed people have little money to spend.

4) When unemployment is **high**, businesses can hire staff easily. There's a good **supply** of labour, so businesses won't have to pay **high wages**. People in work will be extra **productive** to protect their job.

5) If unemployment is **structural** or **regional**, it's not all that easy to hire staff. Unemployed workers often aren't in the **right place** or the **right industry** for the jobs that are out there. They need **training**.

For a long time, there was an inverse relationship between inflation and unemployment — when one was high, the other was low. This was because policies designed to reduce inflation lowered demand, so output fell and workers were laid off. Policies to reduce unemployment increased demand, which fuelled inflation. More recently, supply-side policies (see p.98) have been successful in keeping both low.

Economic Influences

International Trade is the Exchange of Goods and Services between Countries

1) Each country **exports** its own goods and services to other countries and **imports** other countries' goods and services. This international trade means countries can **specialise** in the goods and services where they have a **competitive advantage** (e.g. they can produce them more **cheaply**).

2) Free trade means there are **no barriers** to importing or exporting.

3) **Visible trade** is trade in **physical goods**, e.g. cars, coffee or coal. **Invisible trade** is in **services**, e.g. insurance.

4) The **pattern** of trade **changes** over the years. Firms **enter** and **leave markets**, businesses and countries **gain** or **lose** competitive advantage, **new technologies** come in, patterns of **demand** change.

The Exchange Rate is the Price of a Currency in terms of Another Currency

1) Foreign currency is needed to pay for **international trade** — foreign manufacturers selling goods to the UK need to be paid in their own currency.

2) An exchange rate is determined by the **demand** for a currency and the **supply** of that currency.

3) Demand and supply are determined by international trade. Foreigners **demand pounds** to **pay** for UK exports. UK firms **supply pounds** to obtain **foreign currency** to **pay** for **imports** into the UK. So, **exports** generate a **demand** for pounds. **Imports** generate a **supply** of pounds.

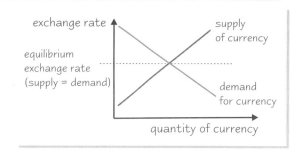

The euro is the unit of currency of several European Union countries. Having a single currency makes trade between these countries a bit easier.

Exchange rate	US price of a UK good costing £6	UK price of a US good costing $6
higher — £1 = $1.50	$9.00 — like, way expensive.	£4.00 — jolly reasonable, what.
lower — £1 = $1.00	$6.00 — like, soooo cheap.	£6.00 — jolly steep, eh.

4) When the exchange rate is **high** (e.g. more dollars to the pound), UK **exports** are relatively **expensive** for foreigners and **imports** into the UK are relatively **cheap** for Brits. A **strong pound** is **bad** for exporters because their goods aren't competitively priced abroad.

5) When the exchange rate is **low**, UK **exports** are relatively **cheap** for foreigners and **imports** into the UK are relatively **expensive** for Brits.

6) **Cheaper imports** mean **lower costs** for UK businesses. **Cheaper exports** should lead to increased **demand** and therefore higher **output**.

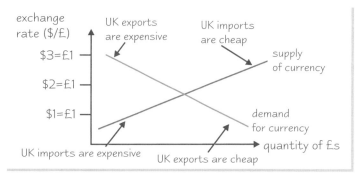

Practice Questions

Q1 Define inflation.

Q2 What is free trade?

Q3 What forces determine an exchange rate?

Q4 When the exchange rate is high, are UK exports relatively cheap or expensive to foreign buyers?

Exam Questions

Q1 What is meant by an 'exchange rate'? (3 marks)

Q2 Assess the likely impact on a large manufacturing company of a projected increase in the rate of inflation. (6 marks)

Inflation is to be expected in the bouncy castle market...

My, but there are an awful lot of potential effects of inflation. It's an economic minefield. This stuff is hard to get your head round at first, but it's really just cause and effect. The table and the graph show you why UK manufacturers get hot under the collar about having a strong pound — it's because it means their goods are harder to sell abroad.

Government Influences

A lot of changes in the business environment are down to the government.
Page 98 is for OCR and Edexcel and page 99 is for AQA, OCR and Edexcel.

The UK Government *Takes Part* in the *Economy*

1) Economies can be **free market** economies, **command** economies, or **mixed** economies.

2) In **free market** economies, the **private sector** does **everything** — even hospitals charge fees to make profit.

3) In **command** economies like the old Soviet Union, the **state** does everything. Nobody tries to make profit.

4) **Mixed** economies like the UK have a **public sector** (the state) and a **private sector** (private business).

5) In mixed economies, the government **takes part** in the economy as a **provider** of goods and services (e.g. state schools, the prison service, the NHS) and as a **consumer** of goods and services (e.g. paying private construction firms to build schools, paying teachers to teach in them).

The Government *Regulates* the *Economy*

1) Governments can introduce **laws** and **restrictions** that govern who can **operate** in a particular market. For example, they can decide who is allowed to run a train service from Maidenhead to London.

2) Government regulation can be a real **constraint** to businesses. It can stop them from making profit in a market.

The Government can *Help Businesses Out*

1) Governments help businesses out by giving **grants** and **loans**.

2) **Regional Selective Assistance** is a **grant** to create jobs in an area with high unemployment. **Regional Enterprise** grants are given to **small businesses** in areas with high **structural** unemployment.

3) **Enterprise Zones** are small areas in inner cities where businesses pay **less tax** and have **fewer regulations**.

4) Government **supply side policies** try to improve the **performance** of businesses and markets, by making it **easier** for them to succeed and make profit.

> **Supply Side Policies**
> - Governments can **cut taxes** and **unemployment benefits** so there's more **incentive to work**.
> - They can **cut taxes** on **business** to encourage firms to **invest** more in production.
> - They can try to improve **flexibility** in the **labour market** by reducing **trade union** power.
> - Governments can try to make it **easier** for businesses to **set up** by reducing bureaucracy.
> - Governments can provide and encourage **training**, which **increases productivity**.
> - **Reducing** the amount of **regulation** helps businesses to compete.
> - UK governments have **privatised** a lot of industries to try and make them more competitive.

The Government's *Economic Policy* influences business

1) **Monetary policy** involves controlling the **money supply** and changing **interest rates**. UK interest rates are now controlled by the Bank of England, independently of the government.

2) **Fiscal policy** involves changing **taxation** and levels of **government spending**. The government is completely in charge of fiscal policy.

3) Taxes can be **direct taxes** like income tax on **individual earnings** and corporation tax on **business profits**, or they can be **indirect taxes** on **spending**, for example **VAT** (Value Added Tax), which we pay on everything we buy, with one or two exceptions like books and kids clothes).

4) Government spending includes spending on **benefits**, spending on **construction** projects and spending on **defence** and **law and order**. Government spending helps businesses — e.g. giving people more benefit means they'll **spend** it in the economy, building a motorway helps **civil engineers** and ordering more fighter planes helps **defence firms** like BAe Systems.

5) Policies to **increase demand** are called **reflationary** policies. Governments **cut taxes** so people have more to spend, and **increase spending** in the economy. Central banks **reduce interest rates** to cut mortgage payments and increase disposable income.

Raising taxes and interest rates is unpopular with voters.

6) Policies to **reduce demand** are called **deflationary** policies. Governments **raise taxes** so people have less money to spend, and **cut government spending**. Central banks **increase interest rates** to raise the cost of borrowing, reduce disposable income and reduce demand.

Government Influences

The **Legal Environment** also affects business

Acts of Parliament set new laws in the UK. The UK is also subject to **European Union Law**, which comes in the form of **directives**. EU law covers working conditions and free trade.

Businesses can be **prosecuted** if they break the **criminal law**. They can be **sued** if they break a **contract**.

①
1) **Consumer law** protects consumers from **unfair business practices** and **unsafe products**.
2) The law affects marketing. The **Trade Descriptions Act (1968)** makes it illegal to put misleading descriptions in advertising. The **Sale of Goods Act (1979)** says that goods must work properly, be fit for purpose and be as described. The **Consumer Protection Act (1987)** means that manufacturers are responsible for harm caused by their products.
3) Consumer law improves the **quality** of products, but also increases **costs** to business.

②
1) **Employment law** both **protects employees** and **restricts** their ability to **strike**.
2) There's **individual labour law** which is about the rights and obligations of individual workers, and **collective labour law** which is about **trade unions** and **industrial relations**.
3) Individual labour law includes the **Sex Discrimination Acts (1975** and **1986)**, the **Race Relations Act (1976)**, the **Disability Discrimination Act (1995)**, the **National Minimum Wage Act (1998)** and the **European Union Working Time Directive** which sets a maximum of 48 hours in the working week.
4) Collective labour law includes the **Employment Acts (1980** and **1982)** which restrict trade union powers, the **Trade Union Act (1984)** which makes trade unions vote before striking, the **Trade Union Reform and Employment Rights Act (1993)**, and the **Employment Relations Act (1999)**.
5) Employment law affects the **costs** and **organisation** of production, but it can improve **motivation**.

③
1) Health and Safety policy is pretty much summed up by the **Health and Safety at Work Act (1974)** which protects **employees**, **customers** and **visitors** to a workplace. It covers safety equipment and clothing, and hygienic and safe conditions.
2) Following Health and Safety requirements **increases costs** for firms, but making workers safe can **reduce labour turnover** — fewer workers get sick or injured on the job.

④
1) **Competition policy** protects **free and fair trade**. It encourages firms to act in the best interests of consumers, and may therefore restrict profits. It also protects smaller firms.
2) The **Competition Act 1998** gives the government more powers against monopolies.
3) The **Office of Fair Trading** investigates restrictive practices such as price fixing, or forcing retailers to stock a large amount of a firm's products. It also investigates firms accused of having a monopoly.
4) The **Competition Commission** can **force** monopolies to **break up** into several smaller firms.

Practice Questions

Q1 Give three examples of ways in which governments can make it easier for businesses to succeed.
Q2 If the government lowers taxes to control the economy, is this a monetary or fiscal policy?
Q3 Give an example of indirect taxation.
Q4 Give two examples of Acts of Parliament which govern trade union activity.

Exam Questions

Q1 Analyse the benefits to a business of locating in an Enterprise Zone. (9 marks)

Q2 Proposed tightening of health and safety legislation
can be an opportunity as well as a threat. Discuss this view. (11 marks)

Everyone likes a nice tax cut...

Governments can do an awful lot to make life easier or harder for businesses. Political parties usually make a big deal about what they're going to do for the economy, for small businesses or for workers — there are lots of votes in keeping the economy running smoothly. You need to know about regulation, government spending, economic policy and the law.

Social Influences

Social pressures and responsibilities affect business. **These pages are for AQA, OCR and Edexcel.**

Businesses have Social Responsibilities

1) **Social** responsibilities are things that a business owes to society. Firms have a particular responsibility to look after the interests of their stakeholders. The firm's stakeholders (see p.84) include **employees**, **customers** and the **community**, as well as **shareholders**.

2) Recent **social trends** have affected firms' **social responsibilities**. These include **environmentalism**, concerns about **business ethics** (see opposite page) and **animal rights**, an increased interest in **health** and **fitness**, more **retired people** and more **single-parent families**.

3) Social awareness has prompted some firms to:

- produce **environmental** and **social audits** — independent checks on the firm's impact on the environment and society.

- change their **products** and **packaging** to be more **environmentally friendly**.

- get raw materials from **fair trade** sources, paying producers in Less Economically Developed Countries (LEDCs) a fair price so that they can earn decent wages.

- change their **marketing** to emphasise **social responsibility**, e.g. the Co-op advertises all its chocolate as fair trade produced.

- change their marketing to emphasise responsibility for **health**, e.g. marketing a food product as a healthy option, low in salt, sugar and saturated fat.

4) **Demographic changes** affect business. For instance, because more women now go out to work, there's an increased need for childcare.

Pressure Groups try to Influence public opinion and government policy

1) **Greenpeace** and **Friends of the Earth** are famous worldwide pressure groups. **Local** pressure groups deal with local issues such as preventing new gravel pits, stopping new roads, or stopping local pollution.

2) How effective pressure groups are depends on their **resources** — the **money** they've got to use on campaigns, the number of **members**, the level of **public support** and their ability to **influence politicians** and the **media**.

3) Firms have **three choices** in dealing with pressure groups. They can **ignore** pressure groups, they can **compromise** or they can do what the pressure group **wants**. The firm's reaction depends on how **forceful** the pressure group is, **media coverage** and the **legality** of whatever the firm's doing that the pressure group is complaining about. It's easier to ignore a small pressure group that no one's heard of, and **hard to ignore** a big pressure group with **media influence** — especially if you're on dodgy legal ground.

Environmental issues can Affect Business Decisions — OCR

1) Current environmental issues include **global warming** and **acid rain** (which are related to emissions from road and air traffic), **energy consumption**, **recycling** and reducing **packaging**, and the disposal of **waste**.

2) Factories often cause **pollution**, but firms don't normally pay **clean-up costs**. Instead, clean-up costs are paid for by society, through **taxes**.

3) Businesses can set **targets** to **reduce pollution**, increase their use of renewable energy sources, increase recycling and reduce packaging etc.

4) The main **business advantage** of taking environmental issues seriously is a good, caring corporate image among consumers and investors. Businesses which work on getting a "green" reputation can attract **new customers** and **increased sales**.

5) A **"green" reputation** can be a competitive advantage, which can push competitors into following suit and behaving in an environmentally friendly way themselves.

6) The main disadvantage is higher **costs**. Green production is almost always quite a bit more expensive.

OCR   OCR

Social Influences

Ethics are Moral Principles of Right and Wrong — OCR & AQA

1) People seem to be more and more concerned about **business ethics** these days.

2) They worry about firms using **cheap labour** in LEDCs (Less Economically Developed Countries), especially **child labour** (some products are made abroad by kids as young as 8 years old). People worry that workers in LEDCs don't have as much protection against **exploitation** and poor working conditions as people in the UK.

3) People are concerned about **environmentally unfriendly products**, and some people feel that businesses aren't **honest** enough about the effect that their products have on the environment.

4) **Animal testing** bothers some people.

5) People are concerned about **obesity**. They may think it's wrong for a business to promote **unhealthy food** — especially by advertising in the middle of kids' TV programmes.

1) Businesses may have an **ethical code** which sets out how they deal with **customers** and **suppliers**, their behaviour towards the **environment** and how **employees** should behave.

2) Acting **ethically** may increase or decrease a firm's profits. Actions which **attract customers** and **investors**, and help to **recruit** and retain **loyal** and **productive employees** all help to **increase profits**. Actions which **cost more** in raw materials, production methods and staff training **reduce profits**.

3) Businesses often find it **hard** to implement ethical policies. Ethical policies can conflict with a firm's existing objectives, including the aim of high profits. Consumers may be **suspicious** of the firm's motives — they may think the firm is just trying to make itself **look** socially responsible to improve its **image**. Employees could **resist** changes to their working practices.

Technology affects Design, Manufacturing and Marketing

1) **Technology** affects **all aspects** of business. Technology has made more high-tech **products** possible, e.g. mobile phones, DVDs, plasma TVs. Computer aided design (CAD) and manufacture (CAM) have changed **production** processes. The Internet has changed **marketing** and **retailing**. Email has changed **communications**.

2) New technology can provide **opportunities** for a firm to **expand**, create **new markets**, improve **production** processes, increase **efficiency**, improve **communications** — all these things increase profitability.

3) Technology can be a **threat**. It could make products instantly old-fashioned, even obsolete. Businesses have to work hard to make sure competitors don't gain a technological advantage.

4) Technology in production is **labour-saving**, which means some employees **lose their jobs**. Employees have to be **trained** to use new technology, and **training costs money**. Some employees resist change.

— OCR & AQA — OCR & AQA —

Practice Questions

Q1 In what ways have some firms become more socially aware?

Q2 Give two examples of ethical policies a firm could have.

Q3 What makes pressure groups effective?

Q4 What is an external cost?

Q5 Why is technology important to business?

Exam Question

Q1 Tastee Limited, manufacturers of a new caffeine-based chewing gum, have been accused of selling a product that may be harmful to health. Describe the ethical and business issues that Tastee Limited must deal with. (10 marks)

This page is free of genetically modified organisms...

Being socially responsible costs money. Whether a business decides to make some ethical change to its policy depends on how much consumers and the media want it to make that change. If businesses can get away with not spending money, they won't spend it. It's as simple as that. Oh, and in case you hadn't noticed, this is the last page. Which is nice.

Answers to Numerical Questions

Section Two — Marketing

Page 31 — Elasticity of Demand

Q1   Maximum of 3 marks available.
If sales fall by 10% after a price rise of 5%, price elasticity of demand
= -10 ÷ 5 = **-2**   *[1 mark for working, 1 mark for answer.]*
Price is elastic *[1 mark]*.

Section Three — Accounting and Finance

Page 35 — Variances

Q1

	Feb cumulative variance	Mar budget	Mar actual	Mar variance	Mar cumulative variance
Revenue	£10k (A)	£110k	£120k	£10k (F)	£0
Wages	£9k (F)	£40k	£39k	£1k (F)	£10k (F)
Rent	£1k (A)	£10k	£11k	£1k (A)	£2k (A)
Other costs	£2k (A)	£5k	£5k	£0	£2k (A)
Total costs	£6k (F)	£55k	£55k	£0	£6k (F)

Page 43 — Costs

Q2   (a)   Maximum of 6 marks available

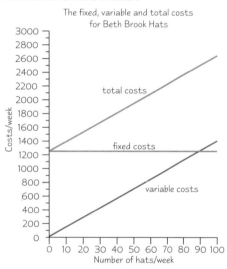

The fixed, variable and total costs for Beth Brook Hats

[1 mark for each correct start/finish point of each line]

(b)   Maximum of 4 marks available.
Costs at 60 hats per week = fixed costs + variable costs
[1 mark]
= 1260 + (60 ×14) = £1260 + £840 = £2100 *[1 mark]*
Revenue = selling price × quantity sold = £50 × 60 = £3000
[1 mark]
Profit = revenue – costs = £3000 – £2100 = £900 *[1 mark]*

Page 45 — Break Even

Q2   Maximum of 4 marks available.
Contribution = selling price – variable costs per unit *[1 mark]*
Contribution = £13 – £5 = £8 *[1 mark]*
Break even output = fixed costs ÷ contribution *[1 mark]*
Break even output = £1000 ÷ 8 = 125 *[1 mark]*

Page 47 — Company Accounts: Balance Sheet

Q2   Maximum 4 marks available.

Total fixed assets			£200 000
Stock		£20 000	
Debtors		£10 000	
Total current assets		£30 000	
Creditors	(£70 000)		
Total current liabilities		(£70 000)	
Net current assets			(£40 000)
Assets employed			£160 000
Share capital			£60 000
Reserves			£100 000
Capital Employed			£160 000

1 mark for each number in bold.

Page 49 — Company Accounts: Profit and Loss and Investment Analysis

Q1   Maximum of 6 marks available.

Revenue		£24 000
Cost of sales		(£9000)
Gross Profit		£15 000
Wages	£3000	
Other overheads	£4000	
Total overheads		(£7000)
Net Profit		£8000
Tax		(£2000)
Dividends		(£5000)
Retained Profit		£1000

[1 mark each for correct gross profit, total overheads, net profit and tax. 1 mark for correct final balancing figure of £1000. 1 mark for identifying the balancing figure as retained profit.]

Q2   Maximum of 7 marks available.
Cumulative cash flow = £10 000 after year 1, £20 000 after year 2,
£35 000 after year 3.
Payback period = 3 years.
[2 marks. 1 mark if working is correct but answer is wrong.]
Accounting rate of return = (average annual profit ÷ investment)
                                            ×100%   *[1 mark for correct formula]*
Average annual profit   = (£10 000 + £10 000 + £15 000 + £20 000
                                       + £20 000 – £35 000) ÷ 5
                               = £40 000 ÷ 5
                               = £8000
[2 marks. 1 mark if working is correct but answer is wrong.]
Accounting rate of return   = (£8000 ÷ £35 000) × 100%
                                     = 22.9% to 1 d.p.
[2 marks. 1 mark if working is correct but answer is wrong.]

Page 51 — Company Accounts: Ratios

Q1   Maximum of 6 marks available.
(a)(i)   acid test ratio = (current assets – stock) ÷ current liabilities
              = (1200 + 800 – 1200) ÷ (400 + 400 + 100) *[1 mark]*
              = 800 ÷ 900 = 0.88 to 2 d.p. = 0.88:1 *[1 mark]*
     (ii) current ratio = current assets ÷ current liabilities
              = (1200 + 800) ÷ (400 + 400 + 100) *[1 mark]*
              = 2000 ÷ 900 = 2.22 to 2 d.p. = 2.22:1 *[1 mark]*
     (iii) net profit margin = net profit ÷ revenue × 100%
              = (4000 ÷ 16 000) × 100 *[1 mark]*
              = 25% *[1 mark]*

Get Marks in Your Exam

This page is about what you're actually marked on in AS Business Studies exams.

You get marks for **AO1 (showing knowledge)** and **AO2 (applying knowledge)**

AO1 marks are for **content**, and **knowledge**. You'll only get about 2 marks for this, whether the question is a short one worth 2 marks, shortish one worth 6 marks or a long one worth 15 marks.

AO2 marks are for **applying** your knowledge to a situation — thinking about the **type of business** in the **question**, the product or service it's selling, and the type of market it's in. You usually get 2-3 marks for this as well.

Don't write too much for short answer questions that **only** test **AO1** and **AO2** marks.

You get marks for **AO3 (analysis)** and **AO4 (evaluation)**

AO3 marks are for **analysis** — thinking about benefits, drawbacks, causes, effects and limitations. Analysis questions usually start with words like "**Analyse**", "**Examine**", "**Explain why**" or "**Consider**".
1) Use your knowledge to **explain** your answer and **give reasons**.
2) With data, say what the figures **mean**, what might have **caused** them and what the **consequences** might be.
3) For top marks, write about **context** — compare a situation with the industry as a whole, or with a competitor.

AO4 marks are for **evaluation** — using your **judgement**. Evaluation questions usually start with words like "**Evaluate**", "**Discuss**", "**Recommend**" or "**To what extent**".
1) **Give two sides** of an argument, and say which you think is **strongest**. Consider **advantages** and **disadvantages** and weigh them up.
2) You don't need a **definite** answer. You can point out that it **depends** on various factors — as long as you say **what the factors are**, and say **why** the right choice depends on those factors. Use your judgement to say what the **most important factors** are.
3) Relate your answer to the **business described in the question** and to the **situation in the question**. Give reasons why **this business** would make a particular decision, and how and why **these particular circumstances** affect their decision.

> **Don't** use **bullet points**. You need to arrange your thoughts in a coherent **essay**. You **can't** get good marks for **analysis** and **evaluation** if you use bullet points.

You get marks for **Quality** of **Written Communication** in essay answers

1) You have to use the **right style** of writing and **arrange relevant information clearly** — write a **well-structured essay**, not a list of bullet points. You need to use **specialist vocabulary** when it's appropriate, so it's well worth **learning** some of the **fancy terms** used in this book.

Jotting down a quick essay plan will help.

2) You have to write **neatly** enough for the examiner to be able to read it. You also need to use good **spelling**, **grammar** and **punctuation** to make your meaning **crystal clear**. Don't worry, you won't lose marks for spelling errors — but if your handwriting, grammar, spelling and punctuation are **so** far up the spout that the examiner **can't understand** what you've written, **expect problems**.

3) Out of the whole paper, you only get **2** or **3** marks for written communication — but remember that if the examiner can't **read** or **understand** your writing, you won't get the **other marks** either.

The **Marks** are **Shared Out** differently by **Different Exam Boards**

1) For **AQA**, all the skills are marked **separately**.
2) For example, an **evaluation** question has some marks for **content**, some for **application**, some for **analysis** and some for **evaluation**. You can **lose marks** for poor content, application and analysis. If you evaluate possible pros and cons **without** specifically stating the **obvious facts**, and specifically **relating** them to the **actual business situation** in the question, you'll **lose out**.

1) With **OCR** and **Edexcel** the mark scheme is like a **ladder** with **AO1 skills** at the **bottom** and **AO4 skills** at the **top**. You get marks according to how far up the ladder you get.
2) Take the example of an **evaluation** question worth **11 marks**. You can get **1-2 marks** for only giving **content**, **3-5 marks** for applying knowledge but not analysing, and **6-7 marks** for analysis but no evaluation. Even if you only give a **half-baked evaluation**, you can actually get **8 marks**. A really **good evaluation** will get you the **full 11 marks**.

Do Well in Your AQA Exam

*This page is all about how to do well in AQA exams. So don't bother reading it if you're not doing **AQA**.*

Each *Exam Unit* covers *2 Core Areas*

1) **Each** unit covers **two areas of the syllabus**. **Unit 1** is Marketing and Accounting, and Finance. **Unit 2** has People in Organisations and Operations Management. **Unit 3** has External Influences and Objectives and Strategy.

2) In the **Unit 1** paper, you get **two compulsory questions**, both with a **short** section of an **article** or a set of figures. One question's on **marketing**, and the other's on **finance**. The questions are worth **25 marks each**, and have four subparts. Each subpart is worth from **2 marks** to **10 marks**.

3) **Unit 2** and **Unit 3** are both based on a fairly long case study — which is pre-released so you can read it and get familiar with it **well before** you get to the exam. Of course, if you wanted to **completely lobster up** your exam and lose lots of marks for being an idiot, you could always leave reading it until you're actually in the exam room. It's up to you. The **case study** contains an **article** describing a business and the **circumstances** it's in. There's also some **data** about the business — **financial accounts** and **sales figures**, etc.

4) Both **Unit 2** and **Unit 3** have **five compulsory questions**. The papers are worth **50 marks** each plus marks for written communication.

5) In Units 2 and 3, short questions are worth about **5-6 marks each**. These short questions will ask you to provide examples and apply facts to a specific situation (AO1 and AO2 skills). Questions asking you to **analyse** a situation and explain reasons for potential outcomes (AO3 skills) are usually worth **8 marks each**. Long questions asking you to **evaluate** different aspects of a situation (AO4 skills) are worth **15 marks**.

Pace yourself — *Don't Waste Time*

1) All three of the papers are **1 hour long**. You can take Units 2 and 3 as two separate 1-hour papers, or you can take it as one 2-hour exam.

2) That means that in Unit 1, you have 30 minutes to answer a 25 mark question with four subparts worth between 2 and 9 marks. That's **not a lot of time** per subpart — and some will take **more time** than others. A 2 mark short question means "bang down a **factual answer** and **move on**". You might have to work out a **numerical** answer for one of the finance questions, and the 9 mark question will be some kind of **mini-essay**. That's where you need to spend your time, not on short questions.

3) In Unit 2, you've got an hour spread between 5 questions. A couple of those will be quite short, and the rest will be fairly long. As a rule of thumb, give yourself about 5 minutes for a short 6 mark question, 10 minutes for a 8-10 mark analysis question, and 20 minutes for a 15 mark essay question

4) If you're asked to give a reason for a decision and **analyse** the reason, all you need to do is give one good reason and then **clearly say why** it's important for the business in the question. That way you get the marks, and you don't waste time. You don't need to write a lot to get marks, you only need to write the **right things**.

5) **Don't waffle** in your essays. Get straight to the point. You've only got about 20 minutes for each of these. If you waste time on one question, you'll be struggling to finish another one at the end of the exam.

An *Example Answer* to give you some tips:

> Explain three types of finance that might be suitable for financing the launch of a new cybercafé business. (6 marks)

This makes good points about loans. →

The new business owner could go to a bank for a loan. They would need to show the bank manager their business plan and prove that they could make a profit. The disadvantage of loans is that they have to be paid back with interest.

It would be good to say that this might not raise enough money. →

Alternatively, share capital could be raised by selling shares. The amount of capital which could be raised can be calculated by multiplying share price by number of shares offered for sale. A new business venture could be set up as a private limited company (Ltd.) and the owners could offer shares to friends, family and managers. They wouldn't be able to offer shares to the public.

This answer covers all three points in equal detail. ←

A third possibility would be venture capital. This would be ideal because large amounts can be raised relatively quickly and the money does not usually have to be paid back as quickly as a loan. Venture capitalists are willing to invest in high-risk ventures such as start-ups as these offer the potential for very high returns if successful. Like the bank manager, a venture capitalist would need to see a business plan.

This answer covers three points, and **applies** them **reasonably well** to the situation in the question. It'd probably get 5 out of 6 marks. To improve, it should apply the answer more to a new business situation — it might be better to write about the owner using their own savings than to write about shares.

Do Well in Your AQA Exam

An *Example Essay* to Give You Some Tips:

> To what extent should a data analysis centre change pay structure in response to high labour turnover? (15 marks)

Don't waffle. Start by making a point.

High labour turnover can indeed be down to low pay, and a pay structure that isn't seen to reward hard work and loyalty. If this were the case, increasing rate of pay and bringing in a scheme of performance-related bonuses and loyalty bonuses or non-financial benefits would tempt employees to stay. Before changing the pay structure, the business should compare their pay with that of rival companies.

Evaluate in comparison to competitors.

It's good to bring in a bit of theory to analyse a potential decision, but you need to relate it to the situation.

The business must make sure that employees' basic needs (the bottom levels of Maslow's pyramid, and the hygiene needs in Herzberg's theory) are being met, before moving on to tackle the higher or motivating needs of achievement, recognition and self-fulfilment. Managers who subscribe to McGregor's Theory X would be likely either to increase pay or to provide performance and loyalty bonuses to bribe workers into staying. Theory Y managers would look for ways to motivate workers.

Evaluate the importance of different factors.

The most important factor in this question is the fact that pay is not the sole reason why employees leave a job. Working conditions may need improving. Health and safety might be an issue with workers sitting at desks in front of computer screens all day. Employees may want more flexible hours than they're currently working.

This shows there are two sides to the argument.

Relate the answer to the business in the question.

It may also be that employees don't have prospects for promotion, and can't see themselves progressing in their current job. This may be because the organisation of the business is too flat — flat organisations provide fewer opportunities for promotion. Restructuring a flat organisation into a tall organisation is an expensive hassle that the business will probably want to avoid. It's also vital that employees understand why the restructuring is taking place. Employees can be resistant to change, especially if there's a pre-existing problem of trust between management and staff.

Give the disadvantages of different options.

Employees may not be able to progress in the firm if they aren't encouraged to put themselves forward for management positions. This can be for two reasons. The business may not adequately train its employees to fill management roles, or it may be that the business actually prefers to recruit externally.

Analyse and give reasons for AO3 marks.

You get AO4 marks for using your own judgement. It can be as simple as this to use your judgement.

There are two key ways to make employees feel more valued. The first is to provide a job enlargement and enrichment initiative that gives workers more tasks, more varied tasks, and more responsibility. The second way is to make sure that management adopt a more democratic style. This approach is difficult to follow without bringing in new managers — most managers have a fairly fixed natural style of management. Bringing in new managers is likely to be too much hassle.

This is too general and not related to the situation in the question.

You can put in a conclusion to sum up your judgement.

In conclusion, the extent to which a business should change pay structure in response to high labour turnover is the extent to which pay is responsible for high labour turnover in the first place. It is vital to research the reasons behind labour turnover before making a decision. Managers could conduct exit interviews when staff leave. They should also listen to staff on a day-to-day basis, and seek open and honest discussion.

It's OK to say "it depends" as long as you say why and point out what you'd need to know in order to find a definitive answer.

This is a fairly good answer. It'd get about **11 marks**. It gives possible **reasons** for high labour turnover, **analyses** them and **evaluates** their advantages, disadvantages and effectiveness.

To improve, it needs to be a **lot more relevant** to the business in the question. The answer barely mentions the specific conditions in a data analysis job at all — it only mentions workers sitting at desks, and it doesn't specifically mention that data analysis is boring in the paragraph on job enrichment. It could also give more of a **personal judgement** — this answer tends to sit on the fence at times.

This answer is also **too long**. It doesn't need to go into so much **detail** of so many causes of high labour turnover. As long as it covers three or four reasons (pay, conditions, management style, boring work) then it'll get the marks for AO1 content skills. Going into more detail is a **waste of time**. It's better to spend time relating the facts to the business, analysing the situation, giving reasons for your points and making judgements between two sides of an argument.

Here's a **sample markscheme** for a 15 mark AQA question:

Content	Application	Analysis	Evaluation
			5 marks: Judgement shown in weighing up value of the strategy to business in question.
3 marks: Good understanding of reasons for labour turnover.	**3 marks**: Relevant knowledge applied in detail to the situation.	**3-4 marks**: Analysis of strategy using theory.	**3-4 marks**: Judgement shown in main part of answer or in conclusion.
1-2 marks: Some understanding of at least one reason for labour turnover.	**1-2 marks**: Some application to situation in the question.	**1-2 marks**: Some use of theory.	**1-2 marks**: Some judgement shown in answer.

Do Well in Your OCR Exam

*This page is all about how to do well in OCR exams. So don't bother reading it if you're not doing **OCR**.*

Each **OCR** *exam unit covers **2** or **3** Core Areas*

1) **Unit 1** is called **Businesses, Their Objectives and Environment** and it covers the Nature of Business, Objectives and Strategy, and External Influences.

2) **Unit 2** is called **Business Decisions** and **Unit 3** is called **Business Behaviour**. **Both** of them cover Marketing, Accounting and Finance, People in Organisations, and Operations Management. Units 2 and 3 also assume you know everything that's covered in Unit 1 — so don't go forgetting about objectives and external influences as soon as you get out of the Unit 1 exam. You can get marks for including that sort of thing.

3) In **Unit 1**, you get **five compulsory questions**, based on a fairly long **case study** which is **pre-released** — you'll have read it already if you're clever. If not, why not read it now. There are two short answer questions worth **2-4 marks**, a longer question worth **9 marks** and two long answer questions worth **14 marks**. The exam takes **1 hour**.

4) **Unit 2** has **four compulsory questions** with a **short** section of an **article** or a set of **figures**. Questions can have subparts (a) and (b) — part (a) is usually a **short** answer based only on facts, and part (b) is a longer **essay** question that asks you to evaluate a business decision or method. There may be questions asking you to work out a **numerical** answer — these are usually worth **4 marks each**. Questions asking you to **analyse** a situation are worth **6-9 marks**. Questions asking you to evaluate pros and cons of a situation are worth **12-15 marks**. The exam takes **45 minutes**, so you don't have a lot of time to write those essays.

5) **Unit 3** is based on a **pre-released case study** — a **different** one to the case study for Unit 1. Unit 3 has **four compulsory questions**. One asks you to **calculate** something based on figures provided. The other three are **essay questions** worth **10-16 marks**. This exam takes **1 hour 15 minutes**.

6) The **case studies** for Units 1 and 3 contain an **article** describing a business and the **circumstances** it's in. There's also some **data** about the business — **financial accounts**, **sales figures**, etc.

An **Example Essay** *to give you some tips:*

> Evaluate the extent to which a manufacturer can operate in an ethical manner, while fulfilling other business objectives. (14 marks)

An ethical business policy can have positive and negative effects on profits. Profit is the main objective of most businesses, so the manufacturer should probably choose aspects of ethical policy which don't cost more than they gain.

An example of changes to production methods would be good.

The manufacturer could try to make sure that all employees in the UK and abroad are treated ethically. This means that they wouldn't be able to exploit cheap labour in Less Economically Developed Countries (LEDCs). This would increase costs, and lower profit. Implementing an ethical policy may also require changes to production methods, which means staff need training. This can be expensive and may be seen as too much effort to be worthwhile.

It's important to state the advantages as well as the disadvantages.

Taking ethical choices can also have a positive impact on profit. If the manufacturer is perceived by its customers as having ethical practices, it will be able to attract customers in preference to competitors who aren't perceived as being ethical. Acting ethically can also help to recruit and retain loyal employees, which reduces recruitment costs.

It's good to relate business decisions to competitor's activities.

Competitor actions are a big factor. If competitors all improve their business ethics, the manufacturer would be at a disadvantage with respect to corporate image if it did nothing. If none of the competitors improved their ethics, the manufacturer would be at a big advantage if it did.

This is a good point, but the answer could get more marks by developing it.

The manufacturer would be more likely to make changes if a powerful pressure group with media influence is pushing for change, e.g. Greenpeace.

Try to write your conclusion without repeating bits from the essay. Use your conclusion to state your judgement.

This conclusion is a bit waffly.

The decision on whether or not to implement an ethical policy depends on the manufacturer's situation. If competitors are improving their business ethics, then the manufacturer should as well. They shouldn't follow ethical practices that are likely to cost a lot of money and conflict with existing objectives. They should take ethical actions which increase profit more than they decrease profit. In short, they should take ethical action if it's worth it financially to do so.

This is a fairly good answer. It'd get about **10-11 marks**. It **analyses** ways of changing ethical policy, and **evaluates** them in terms of their pros and cons and impact on corporate image and profit .

To **improve**, it could **expand and develop** on some of the points made. The answer could give **clearer reasons** why different actions would be good or bad for the business. It could mention pressure from stakeholders. It could say which kinds of business are most likely to draw the attention of pressure groups and the media.

Do Well in Your Edexcel Exam

*This page is all about how to do well in Edexcel exams. So don't bother reading it if you're not doing **Edexcel**.*

The **Core Areas** of the Syllabus are Divided between **Three Exam Units**

1) **Unit 1** is called **Business Structures, Objectives and External influences** and it covers the Nature of Business, Objectives and Strategy, and External Influences. **Unit 2** is called **Marketing and Production**, and it covers Marketing, People in Organisations and Operations Management. **Unit 3** is called **Financial Management**, and it just covers Accounting and Finance. Each unit is tested in a **separate exam**. Each exam is **1 hour** long.

2) **All three** exam papers are based on a **case study**, which is pre-released so you can read it and get familiar with it **well before** you get to the exam. Of course, if you wanted to **completely lobster up** your exam and lose lots of marks for being an idiot, you could always leave reading it until you're actually in the exam room. It's up to you. The **case study** contains an **article** describing a business and the circumstances it's in. There's also some **data** about the business — **financial accounts** and **sales figures**, etc.

3) In **Unit 1**, you get **three compulsory questions**, with subparts (a), (b) etc. Each question is worth **20 marks**. For each question, one subpart will be an "analysis" question worth **7-9 marks** and one subpart will be an "evaluate" question worth **11-20 marks**. Sometimes there'll also be a short question worth **2 marks** asking you for a definition of some technical business term.

4) **Unit 2** has **three compulsory questions** with subparts. Each question is worth **20 marks**. Part (a) is usually a **short** answer based on facts, asking you to work something out or provide an explanation. These are worth **4 marks** each. The rest of the questions are longer **essay** questions that ask you to analyse, consider or evaluate a business decision or method. Questions asking you to **analyse** a situation are usually worth **6-8 marks** each. Questions asking you to write an essay evaluating pros and cons are worth **8-16 marks** each.

5) **Unit 3** has **two compulsory questions** with subparts. Each question is worth **30 marks**. You can be asked to give examples and apply facts to specific situations for **4 marks**. You can be asked to analyse a set of financial accounts for **6-8 marks**. You can be asked to evaluate or assess a method of financial analysis for **10-15 marks**.

An **Example Essay** to give you some tips:

> Michael Adejonwo has used his savings and a small loan to set up a minicab firm in Sheffield.
> Sheffield has two universities and a lively local nightlife. Evaluate the ways in which Michael can promote his business. (12 marks)

Get straight in there. Start by making a point.

Through promotion Michael can inform people about his service, and persuade them to use it. Michael should use a promotional mix of different techniques to promote his service. These promotional techniques need to reflect his limited financial budget, target the people most likely to use the mini-cab service, and take into account that he is promoting a new service which consumers aren't yet aware of.

Give reasons. If you make a statement, say why it's true.

Michael should promote his minicab business through local advertising because he is selling only to a local market. Michael can advertise through the local papers. He can also put notices up in local pubs and bars advertising his business. Advertising in pubs and bars will target his core market of young people out drinking. Placing promotional material in student halls of residence and student union buildings will also reach the student market. Michael could also put cards or notices up in local phone boxes.

The answer relates to the specific kind of business in the question. A general answer won't do.

These are good points, but some of them could be developed a bit more.

Michael could print leaflets and put them through people's doors. If he chose this method, he would need to print a very large number of leaflets, and the cost of printing might well be too high. He would be better advised to limit leafleting to pubs and student buildings.

Michael can try local radio, but he should make sure that he researches local radio stations to find one that his core market listens to.

Because Michael has started his business on a small budget, he doesn't have a lot of money to spend on advertising. He should make sure that his promotional activities are both cheap and good value for money — there's no point in choosing a very cheap method if it isn't at all effective.

There's no conclusion. A conclusion would get this essay more marks.

The student market only exists during term time, so he should make sure he coordinates his advertising with term time. It's especially important to do plenty of advertising at the start of the academic year. If Michael gets his name and phone number well known at the start of the year, students won't bother to look elsewhere for their minicab needs.

This answer mentions competitors, but it would be good to make more of this.

This is a **fairly good answer**. It'd get about **8 marks**, because it analyses and evaluates, and relates the points made to the business situation in the question. The **evaluation** and **judgement** is **limited**, though.

To **improve**, it could make a **clearer judgement** about good and bad ways of promoting a small business (a conclusion would help with this). The answer could give more of the **pros** and **cons** of each suggested method, and say what Michael should do to make the method **more effective** — e.g. it could say that he should make sure bar staff agree to display his advertising in a prominent position.

Index

Index

Index